Teacher's Guide for

SHALOM HEBREW!
Simple Steps to Reading Hebrew

By Ellen J. Rank

Contributing Authors:

Lisa Friedman
Techniques for Learners of All Abilities

Sarah Gluck
Techniques for Adults

BEHRMAN HOUSE

Behrman House, Inc.
www.behrmanhouse.com

Design: AURAS Design

Project Editor: Terry S. Kaye

Contents

Intent and Purpose of *Shalom Hebrew!* Primer

Shalom Hebrew! offers a new, streamlined vehicle for teaching Hebrew reading. With a friendly let's-get-down-to-business approach, *Shalom Hebrew!* takes learners on a quick and direct route to becoming Hebrew readers. The design and content of *Shalom Hebrew!* align with the learning styles of middle schoolers, adults, and/or learners with special needs. Based on *Shalom Uvrachah Primer Express*, *Shalom Hebrew!* retains select key elements of the original approach while incorporating new features to better meet the needs of these specific audiences.

NEW IN *SHALOM HEBREW!*

Shalom Hebrew! focuses on exercises and activities for decoding and building fluency in Hebrew reading. New features in *Shalom Hebrew!* include:

- Each lesson opens with a review of the sounds of all previously learned letters and vowels, and a review of the names of the letters.
- More reading practice is embedded in each lesson.
- A chart listing the name and sound of each vowel appears at the end of the primer.
- New exercises throughout the primer provide opportunities for actively using Modern Hebrew.

In addition to these new features, *Shalom Hebrew!* offers more exercises for:

- Distinguishing look-alike letters
- Matching sound-alike letters, vowels, and words
- Breaking words into chunks (syllabification)
- Practicing reading unusual vowels and consonant/vowel combinations

PRESERVED IN *SHALOM HEBREW!*

Shalom Hebrew! retains many elements of *Shalom Uvrachah Primer Express* that address decoding and reading fluency. The order of letter and vowel introduction remains the same, with more common symbols appearing in the opening lessons. The original key words open each lesson, providing the opportunity for whole-word recognition. And the reading practice found in each lesson has been carried over to *Shalom Hebrew!* Similarly, various *Shalom Uvrachah* exercises, such as the reading of prayer phrases, have been included in *Shalom Hebrew!*

Who Should Use *Shalom Hebrew!* Primer?

MIDDLE SCHOOLERS

Shalom Hebrew! is ideal for middle schoolers (grades five and six). While every learner is unique, middle schoolers can be divided into three main groups: (1) learners who first begin their Hebrew education in fifth or sixth grade; (2) learners who are introduced earlier to Hebrew through an active oral-aural approach; and (3) learners who had difficulty learning to decode and would benefit from starting over.

As described above, the streamlined format and content support quick learning. This is perfect for middle schoolers, who will soon be preparing to become *b'nai mitzvah*. Whether the middle schooler is just entering a class where others began Hebrew reading in an earlier grade, or is part of a group of learners who are in their first year of learning to read Hebrew, *Shalom Hebrew!* is right for that learner. In a matter of a few months, learners can master Hebrew decoding and gain greater accuracy and fluency.

Shalom Hebrew! is a great choice for those who have been learning conversational Hebrew. Incorporating common, modern Hebrew vocabulary into reading exercises allows for quicker mastery of reading. As familiar words appear in lessons, students learn to read using both whole-word recognition and decoding individual letters and vowels.

Techniques for using *Shalom Hebrew!* with middle schoolers begin on page 7.

ADULTS

Adults who choose to learn to read Hebrew are motivated to succeed and usually want to learn to read in a short course of classes. The streamlined, focused structure and content of *Shalom Hebrew!* allow adults to move ahead at a quick pace while still having plenty of opportunity to practice reading new letters and vowels. Many of the key words will be familiar to adults (*b'rachah, havdalah, tzedakah, shofar*) and offer an opportunity for quickly reading—with understanding—new words through whole-word recognition. The design of *Shalom Hebrew!* is fitting for adults; they will not feel that they are learning from a child's primer.

Techniques for using *Shalom Hebrew!* with adults begin on page 20.

LEARNERS OF ALL ABILITIES

Shalom Hebrew! is a helpful tool for teaching reading to learners of all abilities including children with special needs. We all learn and develop differently, and no two students will acquire Hebrew skills in exactly the same way. Our goal is to help each learner meet his or her full potential; teachers will serve their students best by recognizing each one's individual strengths. The content in *Shalom Hebrew!* is focused on learning to decode with a minimum of distracting information. In addition, the primer design is deliberately open and clear with plenty of white space.

Techniques for using *Shalom Hebrew!* with learners of all abilities begin on page 26.

Structure of This Teacher's Guide

This Teacher's Guide takes a three-pronged approach, detailing techniques for using *Shalom Hebrew!* with distinct groups of learners: middle schoolers, adults, and learners with special needs. This approach will assist you in preparing your lessons and designing how your students will use the text as they learn to read.

TECHNIQUES FOR MIDDLE SCHOOLERS

In this section, which begins on page 7, you will be introduced to the varied types of activities in *Shalom Hebrew!* and examine the role and importance of practicing syllabification and actively using modern Hebrew as an aid to fluent and accurate decoding. This section also presents approaches for middle schoolers to complete activities as well as ways for you to introduce key words, and new letters and vowels. There are examples of how you can make collaborative learning a regular part of your class.

You will also find a variety of suggestions for time management that take several factors into consideration, such as the number of days a week you and your learners meet.

TECHNIQUES FOR ADULTS

Beginning on page 20 , you can find suggestions and guidelines for running an adult education class. This includes techniques for welcoming and engaging adults in a Hebrew reading class, Hebrew practice tips, a few helpful points of Hebrew grammar, and ways to introduce the concept of roots.

TECHNIQUES FOR LEARNERS OF ALL ABILITIES

When working with learners with special needs it is important to be mindful of how each one learns best. This section, beginning on page 26, presents techniques and modifications that, while designed to benefit students with specific learning needs, will be useful for *all* learners. It includes ways to build and foster relationships with and among learners, how to teach all learners about diversity among their peers, and how to work with learners with specific learning challenges such as visual or auditory processing difficulties.

RESOURCES FOR ALL LEARNING SITUATIONS, INCLUDING ONE-ON-ONE

Many of the techniques suggested for middle schoolers, adults, or learners with special needs can be adapted for other groups or situations. For example, if you are a tutor, a *madrich* or *madrichah*, or a teacher working one-on-one with a student, you can easily adapt the techniques for that situation. You have the wonderful advantage of giving that learner your undivided attention and differentiating your teaching to his or her specific needs.

ASSESSMENT AND REVIEW SHEETS

In this section you can find sheets to use after lessons 6, 13, 19, and 25 as a review and/or a diagnostic assessment of each learner's reading. There is also a placement test to assess the skills of learners at the beginning of the school year and/or to evaluate the level of those who join the class midyear or appear to be having trouble with certain letters and vowels.

ANSWER KEYS

You can find the answers to activities in *Shalom Hebrew!* beginning on page 37.

USING *SHALOM HEBREW!* WITH MIDDLE SCHOOLERS

SETTING THE STAGE

Display an alef-bet chart and Hebrew vowel chart in your classroom for easy reference. Direct learners to them regularly. Reinforce whole-word recognition by labeling classroom objects, such as כִּסֵּא and דֶּלֶת, with their Hebrew names. Refer to the objects by their Hebrew names.

Before beginning *Shalom Hebrew!* check first with your education director about sending an e-mail to parents describing what they and their child should expect from the class. Mention, for example, the goal of the course (fast and effective Hebrew decoding), how often children will be using the primer in class, and if you will be asking them to practice at home. And, of course, let parents know the best way for them to contact you with any questions or concerns they might have.

LESSON CONTENTS

Each lesson has the following components:

- Opens with a key word
- Introduces one or more new Hebrew symbols (consonants and vowels) found in the key word
- Reviews the names and sounds of previously learned symbols
- Provides reading practice focusing on the new Hebrew symbols
- Includes extensive reading practice that includes new and previously learned symbols
- Presents the English meaning of words that are common in Modern and siddur Hebrew
- Contains activities designed to build reading fluency and accuracy

Note: Unlike the names of consonants, the names of vowels do not appear in the lessons as they are less commonly used. The vowel names are included on the last page of *Shalom Hebrew!* for quick and easy reference. If your learners will be using the vowel names, present the name as each vowel is introduced. Use the names of the vowels regularly and encourage learners to do the same.

PLANNING A LESSON

As you plan, remember that it is helpful to have some established routines. For example, before each lesson post instructions for learners to read specific lines from "Reading Practice" in previous chapters with a partner. Learners will soon get in the habit of looking at the board for instructions and will understand that reading review with a partner is part of their class routine. At the same time, it is equally important to vary how learners use this primer. While attention spans vary, educators often estimate the average attention span as one minute per year of a child's age, plus or minus one minute. If you are teaching eleven-or twelve-year-olds, expect to change the mode of learning every ten minutes or so. This includes shifting among frontal, small group, and individual learning, as well as among kinesthetic, aural, and visual learning. The following pages offer suggestions for presenting the components of the lessons using a variety of approaches.

Decide ahead of time which activities are most helpful and necessary for each learner. You might decide, for example, that the "Word Power" exercises that focus more on comprehension than on decoding would not be appropriate for a child with greater learning difficulties. As you plan your lessons, be sure to identify what is essential for all learners, such as learning the names of the Hebrew letters and reading specific lines in "Reading Practice." Similarly, plan which lesson components can be reserved as enrichment for more advanced readers. You might, for example, challenge the advanced readers to use the words in a "Move It and Use It" exercise in a creative way, such as incorporating the word into a skit. Regularizing this type of differentiated instruction in your lessons will allow for quicker as well as deeper learning: The child with learning challenges could focus on and master core reading skills, while the advanced reader could be building a rich, Modern Hebrew vocabulary.

TIME MANAGEMENT

Your learners are poised to learn Hebrew quickly. Motivated by their upcoming bar or bat mitzvah ceremony, learners recognize the importance of Hebrew reading. The number of months it will take your learners to master Hebrew reading depends on several factors: how many days a week your class meets, how many hours each week can be devoted to Hebrew reading, and your learners' previous experience with Hebrew.

To Master Hebrew Decoding in Three Months

For this rapid pace, you should meet twice a week, completing a full lesson each session (there are 25 lessons). Most lessons introduce two or three new symbols; it is reasonable to expect that learners can absorb and retain that amount of new information. Note that lesson 1 presents six symbols (four consonants and two vowels). Therefore, you may wish to present lesson 1 over two class sessions.

To Master Hebrew Decoding in Six Months

To achieve this pace, plan to complete a full lesson each week. If you meet twice a week, learners can either complete a full lesson one day and then use the second day as a review, or they can complete the first half one day and complete the rest of the lesson on the second day. If you meet one day a week, learners should complete a full lesson each time you meet. As mentioned above, most lessons introduce two or three new symbols; it is reasonable to expect that learners can absorb and retain that amount of new information.

Suggestions for Speeding the Process

As you plan, decide which exercises are essential for your learners. Based on the goals and abilities of students, you may decide to omit certain exercises from your lesson. For example, if learners demonstrate that they can recognize the difference between look-alike letters ד and ר, you could omit "Dalet-Resh Race" on page 36 of *Shalom Hebrew!* which focuses on identifying these letters. If vocabulary acquisition is not a high priority, you might omit an exercise such as "Making Meaning" on page 42, which directs learners to write the English meanings of Hebrew words.

In addition, you may decide to work one-on-one with a learner rather than in a class setting. The personal attention will allow the learner to progress more quickly.

COLLABORATIVE LEARNING

Collaborative learning is a method of teaching in which learners work together so that the group achieves a certain goal. Learning is collaborative rather than competitive. Examples include learners helping one another to complete an exercise in the text or coaching one another on reading new words.

In an environment that supports collaborative learning:

- Learners must feel safe in their groups; they need to know that their classmates will treat them with respect and that it is okay to say that they don't know something, that they need help, or to ask lots of questions.
- The teacher chooses the members of each group. You will want to balance the group—both size and makeup—considering academic as well as social-emotional factors.
- Groups are small enough to allow for everyone to participate actively.
- Each learner knows what to do. Consider assigning "jobs" to different group members. For example, one group member can be assigned the job of reporting the group's answers to the class.

Collaborative learning promotes a more relaxed atmosphere in the class and can make learning much more engaging and fun. Collaborative learning also helps learners to develop their interpersonal skills and to build relationships with classmates. As we become more and more aware of the importance of creating and building relationships within our community, we can better understand the role and impact of employing collaborative learning in the classroom.

It is helpful to think of collaborative learning as a three-step process:

- Present the task to the groups.
- Provide sufficient time for learners to successfully complete the task. Walk around, checking in on groups and answering questions as students are working.
- Debrief.

Using Collaborative Learning to Build Hebrew Reading Skills

THINK–PAIR–SHARE

This method allows for independent thinking, short review with a partner, then checking for accuracy with the full class. To use Think-Pair-Share with *Shalom Hebrew!*:

- Direct learners to independently complete a short exercise.
- After most learners are done, have them turn to a partner and compare their work and agree on an answer.
- Lastly, invite volunteers to share their answers with the whole class.

You might, for example, use Think-Pair-Share when learners are asked to divide a word into syllables.

JIGSAW
Jigsaw allows learners to master a select amount of information and then share their expertise with others.
- Divide the class into small teams. These are called "expert teams" because the team members become experts on a specified set of information.
- Assign each team a task, such as reading a specific row of Hebrew words. Allow the team time for all learners to master the reading. Team members work together coaching one another with the reading.
- Direct learners to move from their expert team to form a new mixed team. Each mixed team will have a member from each of the original expert teams. For example, each member of Expert Team 1 will join a different mixed team so that there will be an Expert Team 1 member in mixed teams A, B, C, and D. (See the chart below.)
- Each person in the new mixed team is an expert on a unique row of words that was practiced with the expert team. Mixed teams then practice reading all the words, helping one another master the reading.

Here is an example of expert teams and how they regroup to form mixed teams.

1 Sarah	1 Becky
1 Gabe	1 Max

Expert Team 1

2 David	2 Jacob
2 Sophie	2 Sydney

Expert Team 2

3 Rachel	3 Emma
3 Jonah	3 Nathan

Expert Team 3

4 Michael	4 Daniel
4 Paula	4 Lara

Expert Team 4

1 Sarah	2 David
3 Rachel	4 Michael

Mixed Team A

1 Becky	2 Jacob
3 Emma	4 Daniel

Mixed Team B

1 Gabe	2 Sophie
3 Jonah	4 Paula

Mixed Team C

1 Max	2 Sydney
3 Nathan	4 Lara

Mixed Team D

Chevruta Reading
Through assessment, using tools such as those found on pages 32 through 36, identify which letters and vowels are challenging for each learner. Create a personalized reading chart for each learner. *Chevruta* (partners) work to help one another gain fluency and accuracy in their reading. Here is an example of a page to give a learner:

Dear Hannah,

This is your customized Hebrew reading plan.

Below is a list of each letter or vowel you will study and the page in *Shalom Hebrew!*

Take turns with your *chevruta*, helping one another to master these Hebrew letters and vowels. Once you feel confident reading them, write their English sounds. Ask your *chevruta* to sign that you can read the letter(s) or vowel(s), and to write the date.

Letter/ Vowel	Page in *Shalom Hebrew*!	English sound	Checked by	Date
בּ	21			
ן	27			
צ	31			

INTRODUCING KEY WORDS, AND NEW LETTERS AND VOWELS

Introducing the Key Word

Each lesson opens with a key word. Your learners will likely be familiar with many of these words; for example, *Shabbat, tzedakah, mitzvah, challah, Torah*. The key word can serve as a launching point for introducing the new Hebrew symbols. You might use the key word as part of a question or piece of information. For example, begin lesson 11 by asking learners if they prefer חַלָה or a bagel. After a quick tally, display and read Word Card #24 or write חַלָה on the board (note that there are *Shalom Uvrachah* Word Cards available at behrmanhouse.com that can be used with *Shalom Hebrew*!). Have learners locate חַלָה on page 43. Call on volunteers to identify the letters and vowels they already know in the word and then to identify the new symbol, ח.

Introducing the New Letter or Vowel

Introduce the new Hebrew symbol in a variety of ways: write or display the symbol on the board, point to the symbol on an *alef-bet* chart, display *alef-bet* flash cards. Say the sound of the letter or vowel. Have learners repeat after you.

Provide different ways for learners to shape the letter as they say the sound. Suggestions include:

- Either individually or with a partner, make the shape of the symbol with your whole body.
- Outline the shape of the letter or vowel using a strand of yarn.
- Write the letter or vowel on a minichalkboard or miniwhiteboard.

As you introduce each letter, teach its name. Inform learners that the sound of each letter is the same as the first sound in its name. Use the name of the letters regularly, and encourage learners to use the names whenever possible.

Invite learners to suggest ways they can remember the symbol's sound (mnemonics). For example, "When I see *dalet*, I think of an open DOOR"; "When I see the "eh" vowel, I think of three EGGS."

Sound the Symbols

Each lesson begins with "Sound the Symbols," which reviews previously learned letters and vowels. As a class, say the sound of each of the letters and vowels listed. Then say the name of each of the letters. If your learners are using the names of vowels, invite the class to identify each vowel by its name. After reviewing this as a class, invite learners to turn to a partner and say the sounds and names of the letters and the sounds of the vowels.

This is a good time to assess how well learners can identify the letters and vowels. Consider asking learners which letters they can easily recognize and which ones they are not sure of. Invite classmates to give suggestions for remembering the sounds of letters and vowels.

TECHNIQUES TO PRACTICE READING

Shalom Hebrew! provides numerous opportunities to practice reading—a key step toward reading accuracy and fluency.

Identifying and Sounding the New Symbols

As each letter or vowel is introduced, direct learners to the lesson's key word in the primer. Ask learners to identify the new symbol in the key word. They might, for example, circle or underline the new symbol. As a class read the key word. Call on volunteers to say the sound of the new symbol.

Write the new symbol on the board. As a class, say its sound. For new letters, add a vowel under the letter. For new vowels, add a consonant. Call on volunteers to sound the consonant-vowel combination.

Hearing and Repeating the Sound of the New Symbol

It is important for new readers to hear the correct pronunciation of consonant-vowel combinations before they try to sound out these combinations themselves. Read the practice syllables and words—one at a time—to your learners, having them follow along in the book and echo what you have read. There are generally five lines of practice after a new symbol is introduced. Vary the way you read the words, for example:

- Read the syllables or words out of order, directing learners to have their fingers or pencils on the word you are reading (they will have to listen to what you are saying and identify the sound to the symbol).
- Read the syllables or words in a fun voice. Call on volunteers to point to the word and to repeat it in their own way. The learner must be pointing to the correct symbols.

After learners have heard and practiced these syllables and words, direct them to take turns reading these practice lines with a partner.

Reading Practice

Each lesson has activities entitled "Reading Practice" with Hebrew syllables and words. You can approach this reading in a variety of ways. Suggestions include:

- Go around the room, having pairs of learners read word parts or words aloud together.
- Direct learners to read in groups of three or four. During that time, you can work one-on-one with individuals in a quiet part of the room. If you have a *madrich* or *madrichah* with you, have them rotate among the groups to ensure correct pronunciation.
- Have learners work in small groups practicing one line at a time. Groups move on to practice the new line once everyone in the group can read the first line.
- Call on various groups, such as people wearing green or those born in the summer, to read a particular line.
- Go around the room, having learners each read one word.
- Direct the entire class to read a word after you say where they will find it. For example, ask them to read the third word on line 4 or the word in line 3 that begins with ל.

For more ideas, refer to the section on collaborative learning (page 9).

To keep learners engaged, remember to vary the activity at least every ten minutes.

USING WHOLE WORDS TO BUILD READING SKILLS

Shalom Hebrew! introduces learners to Hebrew words in a number of ways.
- Each lesson opens with a key word.
- "Reading Practice" includes many Hebrew words, both common and less common.
- In "Word Power" modern and prayer words that appear in "Reading Practice" are defined.
- A number of activities provide the English meanings of Hebrew words and encourage learners to use the Hebrew word in an English sentence.

Decide ahead of time which words learners will practice reading as whole words. As each of these words appears in *Shalom Hebrew!* devote time to having the learners read the whole word. Use word cards to play games that include reading the word quickly. Once a whole word can easily be identified, the learner will be able to fluently read the word without having to sound out each consonant and vowel.

Challenge learners to find the "Word Power" words in the "Reading Practice" lines. For example, direct learners to a particular line, to listen as you read a word, and then to circle that word. Once they find the word, have learners read the word aloud.

Being able to identify and read a word provides a hook for learners to remember the sounds of individual letters and vowels. For example, many learners find it difficult to distinguish between צ and ע. But, if they recognize צְדָקָה, you can show them the whole word, focus on the first letter, and reinforce that צ has the sound "ts."

Reading in general becomes more fluent with greater whole-word recognition. Think about how you read English. If you had to phonetically sound out each word, reading would be very tedious. And so it is for the Hebrew reader.

Suggestions for Building Whole-Word Recognition
- Display key words in the room. Possibilities include posting צְדָקָה on the class tzedakah box, פֶּסַח on a chart of the months and holidays, or מְזוּזָה near the doorpost.
- Place word cards face up on a table with a group of learners standing or sitting around the table. Direct learners to point to the word that you say. Switch by pointing to a word and asking learners to read that word chorally.
- Have four or five whole words printed out. Display one of the words and call on a volunteer to use the word in an English sentence.
- Display seven or eight whole words. Ask learners to close their eyes as you remove one of the words. Call on a volunteer to name the word that was removed.

IDENTIFYING HEBREW SYMBOLS AND SOUNDS

Shalom Hebrew! provides opportunities for identifying Hebrew letters that look alike, as well as letters and syllables that sound alike. For example, see the activities on pages 22, 36, 39, 45, 58, 65, and 86.

Distinguishing Look-Alike Letters

Exercises in *Shalom Hebrew!* focus on the following sets of look-alike letters:

ה ח ת—ס ם—ט מ ס—ב ב כ כ—צ ע—שׂ שׁ—ו וֹ—ז ו

Before learners complete any of these exercises, display each of the letters. Consider having learners practice writing the letters on minichalk- or miniwhiteboards, or having them shape the letters using ribbon or yarn. Call on volunteers to describe the differences between the letters. Ask for clues for remembering the sound of each letter. Clues might include the letter starting a key word that is displayed in the room (for example, דֶּלֶת), or the shape of the letter (for example, the dot over—stressing *o*—the *vav* in וֹ reminds us to say "oh").

After reviewing the letters and their distinguishing features, complete one or two items in the exercise as a class. Once learners understand the exercise, direct them to complete the exercise with a partner or in a small group. When the majority of the learners have finished the exercise, review all or sections of the exercise with the whole class.

Identifying Sound-Alike Letters, Consonants, and Words

Learners identify letters and consonants that sound alike. This is an important skill for developing Hebrew phonological awareness (a sensitivity to and understanding of the sounds of the language) and phonemic awareness (the ability to recognize, isolate, and manipulate those sounds).

In *Shalom Hebrew!* learners will read a group of sounds aloud and then identify and mark the letters or consonants that have the same sound. Similarly, learners will identify and mark letters and syllables that have different sounds. Look for the "Search and Circle" and "Sounds Like" exercises; for example, on pages 5, 14, 24, and 45.

When an exercise is new to students, complete one or two examples with the class. Check that everyone understands how to complete the exercise. If learners are familiar with the type of activity, you can skip doing an example. Consider having learners complete the exercise independently and then reviewing with a partner, small group, or the full class.

PLAYING WITH SOUNDS

Reading tongue twisters and identifying rhyming sounds are entertaining ways for learners to develop decoding skills.

Tongue Twisters

Shalom Hebrew! includes tongue twisters (see pages 13 and 58). Begin with learners practicing the tongue twister independently or with a partner. Partners can then read the tongue twister together. Continued practice reading the tongue twister will build up speed and accuracy.

For fun, invite learners to sing the tongue twister to a familiar tune, such as "Happy Birthday to You." Singing is a great way to build reading fluency. When learners sing, they strive to keep up with the tempo of the group. In addition, research has shown a strong link between music and memory. You can also ask learners to read the nonsense tongue twister with dramatic expression.

Rhyming Sounds and Words

The ability to identify sounds and words that rhyme is an important aspect of developing the ability to recognize, isolate, and manipulate the sounds of letters and vowels.

Exercises in *Shalom Hebrew!* that focus on identifying rhyming sounds and words include:

- Reading a group of words and crossing out the one that does not rhyme
- Reading a group of words and circling the two that rhyme
- Matching a word with other rhyming words

Direct learners to complete the activity with a partner or small group, reading the words chorally. After learners have completed the exercise, invite them to read the rhyming words aloud. Encourage them to read the words with expression, emphasizing the rhyming syllables.

Challenge learners to identify clues for identifying rhyming words. For example, when looking for rhyming words among רֶגֶל–בָּרוּךְ–דֶגֶל–יָדֶךָ, learners could point out that רֶגֶל and דֶגֶל have the same final syllable and share the same vowels ("eh").

See pages 16, 51, 54, 70, 79, and 90 for rhyming activities, usually entitled "Rhyme Time."

WORD BUILDING

The following exercises are designed to enable the reader to identify syllables within a word. The ability to break longer words into syllables makes reading new words much easier. It's key to fluent decoding! For example, when a reader first sees the word קוּפְסָה, it will help if the reader is able to recognize and divide the word into its two syllables. The reader can first decode קוּפ, then blend it with סָה.

Chunk It

"Chunk It" and other exercises give learners the opportunity to practice chunking words into syllables. Introduce these exercises with a conversation about why and how to chunk syllables. Present one example of chunking a longer unfamiliar word, such as אָמְרָה. Ask learners questions, such as: Which is easier, reading the whole word, or reading its components? Why is it easier? What are some clues to look for to indicate the end of a syllable? One goal is for learners to be able to explain that chunking words into syllables turns a long, unfamiliar word into smaller, more recognizable parts and makes reading a new word much more manageable. Another is for learners to be able to split a word into these word parts.

As a class, chunk the first few words presented in each exercise. Allow learners to ask questions about the process. Practice reading the words in chunks and then blended as a whole word. Direct learners to chunk the remaining words with a partner. Then review these as a class. Again, read the word parts and then the full word blended.

See pages 11, 19, 27, and 52 for exercises that practice syllabification.

Word Play

"Word Play" gives learners practice in blending word parts to form full words. In this activity the first player reads the first word part, the second player reads the second word part, and the third player reads the whole word. Consider having small groups do this together, with group members helping one another to master reading each of the words. Then do a quick review and check by repeating the activity, or selections of it, with the whole class.

See pages 16, 25, 39, and 82 for examples of "Word Play" activities.

Double Sh'va

A number of activities focus on words that have a double *sh'va*. Learners gain awareness that when they see a *sh'va* under two consecutive letters, the first *sh'va* is not sounded and indicates the end of a syllable. Learners practice dividing the word into word parts, as well as blending the word parts to decode a longer word. These activities may be completed individually, or with a partner or small group, and then reviewed as a class.

See pages 83 and 94 for activities that practice double *sh'va*s.

BRINGING HEBREW TO LIFE

Throughout *Shalom Hebrew!* learners have the opportunity to actively use modern Hebrew words. The modern Hebrew vocabulary focuses on common classroom and holiday words. For those learners who have been introduced to the language through oral Hebrew, many of these words will probably be familiar. Many exercises in the primer are designed for learners to use these modern Hebrew words.

Consider adding these Hebrew words to your everyday conversation and class environment. For example, you might ask a learner to take out an עִפָּרוֹן (pencil) or to close the חַלוֹן (window). Or you could direct a learner לִקְרֹא (to read) or לִכְתֹּב (to write). Hearing or actively using a word with regularity provides learners with a hook for reading the word. The word is no longer a cluster of syllables, but rather a word with meaning.

Move It and Use It

Through the "Move It and Use It" activities, learners use modern Hebrew words in a variety of ways. Learners:

- Practice reading words and then connect each word to its matching illustration. *Shalom Hebrew!* often uses this direct method instruction, in which vocabulary is acquired through pantomiming, or using real-life objects or other visuals. This is in alignment with direct method instruction for language acquisition.

- Follow instructions that include Hebrew words. For example, one exercise directs learners to take a step קָדִימָה (forward) after reading each line correctly, and to draw a קַו (line) under the food we eat on Passover.

- Practice reading words and then act out the word. Classmates guess the word.

- Practice reading a phrase, such as יָדַיִים עַל רֹאשׁ (hands on the head), then act out the phrase.

- Practice reading a list of Hebrew words. The English meaning of each Hebrew word is included in the exercise. Using that list, learners circle the Hebrew names of items they see in the classroom. Then they touch each item in the class as the teacher, or another classmate, says its name.

- Read and use words such as קָדִימָה (forward) and (left) שְׂמֹאלָה to direct classmates where to walk in the classroom.

- See pages 25, 31, 36, 42, 55, 61, 63, 70, 72, 75, 79, and 87 for "Move It and Use It" activities.

SHABBAT AND HOLIDAY VOCABULARY

Hebrew words associated with Shabbat and holidays are introduced for reading practice throughout the primer. Reinforce whole-word recognition and build learners' reading fluency by writing these words in Hebrew, rather than English, whenever possible. For example, if the class is listing items found on a Shabbat table, write or display חַלָּה, rather than *challah*.

SPECIAL READING RULES

There are a number of vowels, letters, and letter-vowel combinations that are especially challenging to new readers. *Shalom Hebrew!* brings these to the learners' attention and provides opportunities for the reader to practice decoding words with these symbols.

The primer includes exercises that focus on the following reading rules:

- When ֵ , ֶ , and אָ are followed by the letter י at the end of a word, say "EYE" as in "SHY" (שַׁי)
  (בְּוַדַּאי ,סִינַי).
- When יו ָ comes at the end of a word, the letter י is silent. (דְּבָרָיו).
- The vowel ֳ is always pronounced "OH." (חֳדָשִׁים)
- When the vowel ָ comes before the vowel ֳ , both vowels are pronounced "OH." (צׇהֳרַיִם)
- The letter ה is pronounced "H," but when ה comes at the end of a word and has no vowel under it, it has no sound. (בָּכָה)
- Most of the time וֹ has the sound "OH" (צֹו). Sometimes וֹ is pronounced "VO" (צְוֹ עֲוֹ). *Hint:* If there is a vowel under the letter before וֹ, then וֹ is pronounced "VO." (מִצְוֹת)
- When the vowel וֹ is followed by the letter י at the end of a word (וֹי), say "OY" as in "BOY." (אוֹי וַאֲבוֹי)
- Some dots do double duty. They tell you that the vowel sound is "OH" *and* whether the letter שׁ makes a "S" or a "SH" sound. (מֹשֶׁה)
- When חַ appears at the end of a word, say "ACH" as in "KO-ACH" (כֹּחַ).
- When the vowel וּ is followed by the letter י at the end of a word, say "OOEY" as in "GOOEY." (וְדוּי)
- There are five letters that have a different form when they appear as a final letter. (כ-ך ,מ-ם ,נ-ן פ-ף ,צ-ץ)
- As learners are introduced to each of these special reading rules, invite them to ask questions so that they better understand the rule. Read the words presented in these exercises aloud to the class so that they hear the correct pronunciation. Have the learners repeat the words after you. Then have learners practice these words with a partner or in small groups.

LEARNING AT HOME

Review and practice at home will help learners hone the Hebrew decoding skills and vocabulary they acquire in school. However, whether or not to assign homework is a decision best made by your school administration. If learners will be practicing at home, they can visit www.behrmanhouse.com and click on "Students" for free reading practice.

ASSESSMENT

Ongoing assessment will help you track whether learners are mastering the material and plan remediation accordingly. You probably will not be able to assess every learner on every lesson. Therefore, the assessments provided on pages 32–36 are cumulative (lessons 1–6, 7–13, 14–19, and 20–25). Learners that are having difficulty should be evaluated more frequently, at least after every other lesson. They will also likely benefit from one-on-one attention and coaching.

You can use the "Placement Test" on page 32 to assess the skills of learners at the beginning of the school year and/or to evaluate the level of those who join the class midyear or appear to be having trouble with certain letters and vowels. You can also use it toward the end of the year to assess the skills of the entire class or grade.

We recommend the following procedure for assessment:

- Provide learners with a master copy of the assessment sheet. On a separate copy, which you should keep for each learner's records, make notes about learner's errors. Ask each individual to read the words from one lesson without stopping. Put a check next to each word that he or she reads correctly. If the learner makes mistakes on the first three items, or on five items total, stop the assessment and remediate. For example, allow the learner to practice this item with a tutor or *madrich/madrichah*. If the learner demonstrates reading fluency, have him or her continue reading each set of words for the lessons the class has studied.
- Mark a slash (/) through any item on which the learner makes an error and write a phonetic equivalent of the mispronunciation above the slash; for example, *mal* instead of *tal*.
- If the learner skips an item, put a slash (/) through it, but without a phonetic note.
- If the learner adds a sound, such as an extra vowel, draw a circle and write the addition inside it, for example: אֵת.
- Do not let learners see what you are writing. Accept self-corrections, but do not give feedback until the learner has completed the evaluation.

Assessments can also reveal areas that the class should review as a whole. If you see that several learners are having difficulty with the same item—for example, confusion of certain look-alike or sound-alike letters—a classroom or small group review may be beneficial.

CLASSROOM GAMES

Games can add variety and energy to your classroom. They reinforce learning and capture learners' attention through a fun, lively medium. As you plan to use the games below, or others you may develop or choose to use, keep the following considerations in mind:

- Choose games that contribute to improving specific skills and reading fluency—games that have pedagogic value.
- Use games that move quickly. Don't spend more time on a game than it deserves.
- Stop when learners' interest begins to wane.
- Choose games appropriate to the age group.
- Use games that are easy to follow and organize. Explain rules clearly. Avoid complicated directions.

You want learners' attention focused on the skills being reinforced, not on rules.

- Maintain control of the class.
- When playing a game with the entire class, make sure that all learners are actively involved and can experience success.

Alef-Bet Algebra

Display letters that have been taught along with their Hebrew numeric value. (You can find the numeric value of Hebrew letters online.) Divide class into teams of three to four players. Write an equation on the board. For example, $\_\_\_ = \mathrm{מ} + \mathrm{ת}$

Once a team solves a problem, they must read it aloud, using the proper name for each Hebrew letter. In this example, the team would say, "*Tav* plus *mem* equals 440." The team earns two points for being the first to solve the problem. If other teams have solved the problem, award them each one point. The team with the most points is the winning team.

Alef-Bet Workout

To reinforce the shape of Hebrew letters (and strengthen some muscles), learners write a Hebrew letter in the air with their feet. Invite volunteers to call out the names of the letters.

Odd Word Out

Write four words on the board. Three should be related, and one should be unrelated. Challenge learners to circle the "odd word out." For example, three of the four words rhyme, or three of the four words end in a final letter.

Old Favorites

Games such as Baseball, Memory, Bingo, and Hangman can be used to reinforce reading skills.

Reminder: In order to progress quickly through *Shalom Hebrew!* we recommend that you select games that are purposeful in driving learning.

PART 2

USING *SHALOM HEBREW!* WITH ADULTS

Shalom Hebrew! is ideal for use with adults, especially those with busy schedules who want to learn to read Hebrew fast and efficiently. The streamlined content and presentation allow adults to progress quickly while still having plenty of opportunity to practice. Many of the key words will be familiar to adult learners and offer an opportunity for reading new words—with understanding—through whole-word recognition.

WELCOMING AND ENGAGING ADULTS

Celebrate Your Students

Jewish learning is meant to be enjoyable. Our tradition teaches that Torah is as sweet as honey. Help your adult learners start their Hebrew journey on the right foot by welcoming them warmly and establishing a safe, nonjudgmental learning environment in the classroom or other designated space. Affirm this positive and significant step in their Jewish learning and cheer them on.

Establish a Classroom Community

Adult learners often come with baggage. Set it down and unpack it together. Common burdens might include: a negative experience with Hebrew or some other aspect of formal Jewish education; an unpleasant encounter with a Jewish role model or professional; no formal Jewish education; a history of feeling ignorant in Jewish settings, e.g., at synagogue services or the Passover seder; or no Jewish background at all. Maybe their Hebrew studies were dry, boring, or unimaginative. Perhaps the significance of Hebrew to the Jewish people was never explained or demonstrated. Help lighten the load by getting to know each other. Invite everyone to share something about their background and why they are learning Hebrew. Be open, friendly, and encouraging. Sharing both positive and negative feelings about these experiences will help your students see that they are not alone. Acknowledging these challenges openly and in a nonjudgmental manner will help establish an atmosphere of trust and foster a sense of classroom community.

Acknowledge the Effort

Your students have made a commitment to Jewish learning by signing up for and coming to class. Again, this is to be celebrated. For many adults, choosing to devote time in their busy lives to their own learning is a big, sometimes daunting, step. Among the many roles you will play are teacher, advisor, cheerleader, and friend. Make sure to acknowledge that their Hebrew studies are for them, not to please you. Your responsibility is to support your students in their efforts.

Keep Up Morale

Keep your finger on the pulse of the group. In addition to listening carefully and watching the group for a general sense of how everyone is doing, also watch for facial cues or body language that might suggest that someone is uncomfortable or struggling with the material. Check in regularly with the group as a whole and with everyone individually. Make sure that no one leaves a session with an unresolved question or issue. If something requires further discussion, make an appointment to follow up as needed.

Stay in Touch

A weekly group e-mail that reports on what you covered in class and looks ahead to the next session can go a long way toward keeping your learners connected and on track. Everyone learns at a different pace, and some learners may feel that they are falling behind no matter how hard they work. Others may feel guilty for not studying between classes. Sometimes life just gets in the way. Absences are inevitable, and learners may be tempted to drop the class. Sending an e-mail a day or two after each session goes beyond the simple relaying of information. It can be encouraging to those who may feel insecure about their abilities while also conveying that you are available to help both in and out of class.

Set Attainable Goals

Establish standards. Set the bar high, but not so high that it is an obstacle to success. The primary goal is to help your learners learn to decode Hebrew accurately. Fluency will come with practice; some will achieve it sooner than others. The key is to practice consistently—an attainable goal for anyone.

A secondary, parallel goal is to prepare your students to read Hebrew by enriching their decoding work with key Hebrew vocabulary, rudimentary grammar, and general Jewish enrichment. (See more below.)

Have Fun!

Your passion for Hebrew and the pleasure you take in your teaching will be contagious. Your students will understand that learning to read Hebrew can be a joyous activity!

HEBREW PRACTICE TIPS

Adult learners are simultaneously at an advantage and at a disadvantage when learning a new language. On the one hand, they are able to process information quickly and to store useful information for future reference. On the other hand, they are just beginning to learn the mechanics of Hebrew decoding and are not yet proficient. As challenging and intimidating as it might feel for children to learn a new set of characters and acquire basic skills in another language, it may feel all the more so for adults, precisely because they have attained skills and achieved competence in other areas of their lives.

You can help your new Hebrew readers relax by explaining that Hebrew is accessible to everyone and that everyone has to start somewhere. Make a point of explaining that the first goal is to recognize letters and vowels in order to become skilled decoders and, later, fluent and comfortable readers. Note that while they will be reading Hebrew aloud in class (and, you hope, at home), they will not be learning how to speak Hebrew. (That can come later, if they choose.) In other words, active pronunciation, not active language production, is the emphasis at this first level of study.

Nevertheless, there is much to assist and enrich their learning:

- Tips on how to navigate a page and tackle a word, phrase, or passage are helpful (see below for more on mnemonics, special marks, etc.).
- Learning to recognize Hebrew roots allows even beginners to discern meaning in words.
- Key vocabulary enhances the ability to understand the gist of a phrase or passage.
- Grammar can help learners move beyond mere phonetic reading to being able to see and understand words and phrases. Grammar is not something to be feared. It is useful and should be embraced.

HEBREW DECODING TIPS

Learn to Look Both Ways

Guide your learners to look right for Hebrew and left for English. This may seem obvious, but remember that among your students there may be those who have had no exposure whatsoever to Hebrew. For them, Hebrew truly is a foreign language. Moreover, a mixed English-Hebrew textbook may be confusing initially.

Shalom Hebrew! will help train your learners' eyes with its placement of key words and new letters and vowels on the right as they are introduced at the beginning or in the middle of a lesson.

Keep Your Eye and Your Finger on the Page

Using your finger (not a pen or pencil) to follow along with each line may seem obvious, but it prevents learners from losing their place, which can fluster them. It is a good habit to get into.

Avoid Transliteration

Note that transliteration can be helpful when used selectively (when introducing the vowels or writing names of prayers on the board, for example). Otherwise, avoid it, as it can hinder the Hebrew learning process. Some learners will want to write transliterations in their books. Explain that though they may feel they need it now, they will not later on. Encourage them to be patient and discourage them from developing an unhelpful habit.

Name Letters and Vowels

Note that it requires fewer words to name something than to describe it. While the names of new letters are introduced at the beginning of each lesson, the names of the vowels are not. You can find the names of the vowels in the chart at the back of book. Introduce the names of the vowels from the beginning. Each time a new vowel is introduced, teach it by referring to the chart. Have the learners write the name of the vowel in transliteration next to its symbol on the page. As noted above, this is one of the few places where transliteration can be helpful.

Pay Attention to the Space between the Words

A great pianist once said, "The notes I handle no better than many pianists. But the pauses between the notes—ah, that is where the art resides." Words are the notes of language, and the space between them its pauses. You can help your learners work toward becoming fluid and expressive Hebrew readers by helping them pay attention to the space between words. Set the pace for reading out loud as a group by counting 1-2-3 in Hebrew: "*Achat, sh'taiyim, shalosh.*" The pace will vary depending on what is being read. Do this every time you practice decoding together. This also helps keep the group together when reading in unison.

Use Mnemonics

Mnemonic clues can help learners remember the letters. A few examples are "*bet* has a bellybutton," "*lamed* looks like lightning," "*sin* is never right." Without spending a lot of time on this, challenge your learners to come up with their own mnemonic devices and have fun with it.

Mark the Text

Feel free to come up with special markings that you think might help your learners "see" words and phrases more easily. Two suggestions are to draw an arch over two letters to indicate that they are to be blended (e.g., over the *bet* and *resh* in *b'rachah*; over the *tzadee* and *dalet* in *tzedakah*), and enclosing two or more words in parentheses to indicate that the words comprise a phrase and are to be read with less space between them (e.g., *Shabbat shalom, bat mitzvah*).

Drill Creatively

Every lesson in *Shalom Hebrew!* includes "Reading Practice" exercises. Encourage your learners to review these at home, but make sure you introduce and drill them in class. This repetition and reinforcement is essential. Avoid going around the room with each learner reading out loud. Drilling does not have to be boring, and it should never make a learner feel that he or she has been put on the spot. While it may be necessary from time to time for learners to read aloud individually, in general focus more on reading as a group. You can make it lively and fun. As you get to know your learners and become more familiar with the book, enjoy developing your own techniques. Here are a few suggestions to get you started.

- *Read and repeat.* Pronounce a word and have the class repeat it in unison. Do this with every word in a line. This serves the dual purpose of making sure your learners are introduced to the correct pronunciation of each word, while also providing them the opportunity for active listening and active, correct pronunciation. Do this once for lines with simple words and then move on, or, where the words are more challenging, repeat the line as many times as needed.

- *Read each line in unison.* Set a comfortable pace—not too fast, not too slow. This will help you gauge everyone's ability. Adjust the pace as needed. This not only will accomplish the drill but also help all learners feel that their needs are being noticed and met.

- *Ask questions about the key words.* Intersperse some quick visual activity into the reading practice by asking questions about key words in a line. ("Did you notice a familiar word in the line? What is it? How did you recognize it? Do you know what it means? How many times does it appear? Can you figure out the root letters?") This gives learners a break from the rote aspect of drilling while giving them the opportunity to see and hear the words differently and to make associations between the words on the page and their own Jewish experiences (for example, hearing the word in services or in a familiar life-cycle ritual or holiday celebration; recognizing the word in the context of a snippet of melody from a prayer or song).

- *Drill the words.* For lines with challenging words that learners may be having difficulty with, drill the line by repeating each word several times, then go back and read the whole line together.

- *Do "rapid-reading racing."* Use exercises that are arranged in a neat grid for "rapid-reading racing."

Have fun reading each line across (right to left, of course). Then, starting with the rightmost column, read vertically top to bottom, then vertically bottom to top. Avoid reading anything left to right. Even though this reading drill takes a few minutes, it can liven the pace because it moves quickly.

Do Written Exercises Orally

Consider doing "Search and Circle," "Sounds Like," "Word Power," and other similar exercises orally. Adult learners don't need to spend time on circling, drawing lines to match, and so forth, but instead should focus their time and effort on rapid visual intake, pronunciation, and making associations.

Incorporate Key Cultural Words for Recognition and Acquisition

Decoding practice can be a great entry point to learning vocabulary. For example, after reading out loud from the textbook, you can ask learners to read a line silently to themselves and see if they are able to identify the "real" Hebrew word in it (e.g., *bat*). It's likely that someone will be able to do this. Ask them to explain how they identified the word. Was it by word recognition? By association with *bat mitzvah*? This provides a good opening to discussing how they, even as beginning Hebrew decoders, can trust their ears and make associations with general Jewish knowledge they may have. (Of course, be sensitive to the fact that not everyone has a Jewish background or has been exposed to Hebrew.)

Provide Online Support

Adult Hebrew learners may be reluctant to practice their reading outside of class because they may not have any way of knowing whether or not their pronunciation is correct. Knowing that online support is available can be an incentive to practice. Encourage them to use the freeware at www.behrmanhouse.com, especially the "Click-n-Read Hebrew at Home," which is a companion to the *Shalom Uvrachah* primer. They can find this by clicking on the "Students" section of the website home page—www.behrmanhouse.com. Another easy and effective way to provide audio support is for you to record selections from *Shalom Hebrew!* by creating audio clips on your computer or mobile device and e-mailing them to your students or posting them on your institution's website.

HEBREW SYLLABIFICATION

Arch It

Identify syllables by drawing arches over them (see "Chunk It" in lesson 2).

Accenting in Hebrew Words

This can be introduced as early as lesson 5 (page 22, line four of "Bet-Vet, Kaf-Chaf Karate," fourth word, *ma-LACH-ta*), or wait until lesson 6, when the heritage word *v'-a-HAV-ta* is introduced.

Sh'va

Having learned how to divide words into syllables, students can now learn the rules that govern the *sh'va* vowel (introduced in lesson 4). Useful *sh'va* exercises also can be found in lesson 13, page 52, "Loud and Louder"; lesson 22, bottom of page 83, "Double Sh'va Toss"; and lesson 25, top of page 94, "Double Sh'va Relay."

Chataf Vowels

Chataf-patach is introduced in lesson 5. The "Reading Rules" for *chataf-kamatz* can be found in lesson 16, bottom of page 61.

INTRODUCING HEBREW ROOTS

The end of lesson 1 is a good place to introduce the concept of the three-letter root in Hebrew (introduced for younger students in lesson 25, page 93). Here are a few easy steps to follow.

- Explain that many words in Hebrew are derived from three-letter (occasionally four-letter) roots.
- Roots become words when they are combined with vowels and certain other letters according to the rules of Hebrew grammar.
- Use שַׁבָּת as the example and write it on the board. Write clearly in block letters. Make sure that everyone can read your handwriting.
- Explain again that Hebrew roots generally, though not always, comprise three letters, and that שַׁבָּת is derived from the three-letter root shin-vet-tav, which expresses the basic meaning of "ceasing," "stopping," or "resting."
- Write shin-vet-tav on the board.
- Circle the three root letters in שַׁבָּת to make it easier for your students to see them.
- Note that the letters of a root always appear in the same sequence in the words that are derived from it.
- Now write the word שָׁבַת on the board.
- Ask students to identify the root letters while you circle them.
- Ask if anyone can note the difference between שָׁבַת and שַׁבָּת. (Learners will likely note the difference in the vowels and in the bet/vet. Tell them bet and vet are essentially the same letter.)
- Explain that it is the vowels (and certain elements of grammar that can be explained later on, like the dagesh, the dot in letter) that create word patterns and make a noun (Shabbat) and a verb (shavat) from shin-vet-tav.

Ask students the relevance of "ceasing," "stopping," or "resting" in the context of the Creation story. Knowing the linguistic origins of the word שַׁבָּת can help us understand that the Sabbath is a day in which we make an effort to cease or stop what we do on the other days of the week, and that we do this in order to refresh ourselves, as God did according to the Torah on the seventh day after completing the work of Creation.

From this we return to two important lessons noted above:

1. Learning to recognize Hebrew roots allows a beginning Hebrew reader to discern meaning in words.
2. Learning key vocabulary enhances a beginning reader's ability to understand the gist of a phrase or passage.

Helping your students learn how to recognize roots and introducing common roots throughout their course of study will help them immeasurably in their efforts to become fluent and comfortable Hebrew readers. Even though they are just beginning their studies, recognizing roots can add a layer of understanding that will connect them more deeply to the Hebrew words and phrases they encounter most frequently—the Hebrew of worship and prayer, of holiday celebrations, of ritual and life-cycle events—making possible a richer and more vibrant Jewish experience.

PART

3

USING *SHALOM HEBREW!*
WITH LEARNERS OF ALL ABILITIES

Every student learns and develops differently, and no two learners will acquire Hebrew skills in exactly the same way. Our goal is to help each learner meet his or her full potential; teachers will serve their learners best by recognizing each individual's strengths. *Shalom Hebrew!* offers a broad variety of activities for learning to decode Hebrew that can be modified for different types of learners. Consult with your school's director to learn more about each learner's specific learning needs.

The techniques and modifications listed below, while designed to benefit learners with specific learning needs, will be useful for *all* learners.

GENERAL APPROACHES FOR LEARNERS WITH VARYING ABILITIES

Build Relationships with Your Learners

- Reach out to learners and their parents before the school year starts by sending home a letter or e-mail or by calling to introduce yourself.

- Show a personal interest in learners and their lives. Find ways to weave their interests into lessons in authentic ways. For example, use baseball when you know a learner likes the game. Ask, "What sound does *bet* make?" "B." We hear the sound *bet* in *Shabbat* or in the words *baseball* or *bat.*"

- Establish that fair doesn't necessarily mean equal; fair means that every learner gets what he or she needs to be successful. As teachers, we must treat learners fairly, not necessarily equally.

Foster Relationships among Learners

Begin the first class with a "get-to-know-you" game or mixer, but don't stop there. Add trust-building activities to your lessons periodically throughout the year to keep the connections strong and foster the ongoing development of new connections.

Here's an activity to foster relationships.

Have a conversation about the power of words. Discuss how easily words can hurt and how it is just as easy to use words to lift someone up. For example, when we laugh at children who stumble when reading Hebrew, we can hurt them. When we compliment others for reading well or showing improvement in reading Hebrew, we can help them feel good about themselves.

Brainstorm together positive words that might be used to describe a friend or someone you care about. Steer children away from generic words like *nice* and *fun*. (*Examples: kind, generous, funny, helpful, outgoing*)

Teach about Diversity

Learners of all abilities benefit from a lesson and/or discussions about diversity to help them recognize that each of us is unique and that each of us has strengths and gifts to offer.

Here's an activity to teach about diversity.

Materials: 1 small white egg, 1 extra large white egg, 1 brown egg, 1 or 2 eggs (any color) with marks or "imperfections," 1 or 2 eggs (any color) with slight cracks (not enough to break the egg open).

Display all of the eggs. Ask learners to describe the various eggs, noting similarities and differences. Guide learners to point out the following differences: size of eggs, color of eggs, markings, cracks. Ask learners to guess what the eggs look like inside.

Crack each egg open in a separate bowl. Compare how, despite the exterior differences, all of the eggs are the same on the inside. Emphasize the ways that we underestimate people and their abilities when we judge them only by the way they look.

Discuss how this might positively change the way we treat people in the future. (*Examples: learners may be kinder to others, learners may stand up for others who are being picked on, learners may recognize that everyone has something of value to offer*)

Some older children may feel comfortable sharing their own challenges and/or special needs as a part of this conversation. This could be the perfect opportunity to discuss such "invisible disabilities" as dyslexia, processing disorders, anxiety, etc.

ADDRESS LEARNING STYLES

There are three main types of learning styles. They are:
- *Visual learners.* They learn best by seeing. When information is presented in the form of print, graphs, maps, or actual demonstrations, they are better able to retain the information.
- *Auditory learners.* They learn best by hearing and speaking. Auditory learners often need to talk about the main points of the material being presented with a second person. They learn best through discussion and explaining the topic to people who do not understand it.
- *Kinesthetic/Tactile learners.* They learn best by touching and doing. Hands-on activities are their preferred mode of absorbing information.
  Learning styles are not fixed. However, engaging a learner in the style he or she prefers will enable him or her to find success more quickly.

As an activity in self-awareness, identify your own learning style to better work with your students. You may choose to complete a learning styles inventory (there are many online), or you may already be aware of the way that you learn best. Keep in mind that regardless of your own learning or teaching style, you need to cater to students' needs.

TECHNIQUES FOR LEARNERS WITH SPECIFIC LEARNING CHALLENGES

In order to use *Shalom Hebrew!* effectively, it will be helpful for you to know your learners' specific learning challenges. That way you can craft techniques that respond to the challenges head-on.

For Learners with Attention Issues

- Seat the learner close to you to minimize distractions, such as pencil tapping or noise from the hallway.
- Consider allowing learners to use music (wearing headphones) to tune out background noise, when appropriate.
- Ensure that all directions are clear and give them both orally and visually, by writing them on the board or handing out written directions on paper. Repeat directions as needed.
- Privately establish a refocusing system with the learner, such as a gentle tap on the shoulder or your approaching his or her desk.
- Allow the use of fidgets (small manipulative objects) to help learners focus. Provide guidelines to the class about the use of fidgets, and monitor their use to ensure that they do not become distractions themselves.
- Help learners organize their supplies.
- Provide an extra copy of *Shalom Hebrew!* for use at home.
- Ensure homework assignments are written down or email them home.

For Learners with Auditory Processing Issues

- Minimize noise and distractions (see above).
- Have the learner repeat directions back to you to ensure understanding.
- Consider allowing learners to listen to recorded directions so that they can repeat as frequently as needed. Teachers might create MP3s of the directions and load them onto a learner's phone or listening device or use a voice recording app on a smart phone or tablet.
- Allow the learners to watch videos with content information to enable them to move through the material at their own pace, repeating as necessary. For example, you might create a video of yourself teaching key words and new letters and vowels introduced in *Shalom Hebrew!* so that learners can review the material as needed.

For Learners with Visual Processing Difficulty

- Read written directions and other content information aloud.
- For individual seatwork, allow the learner to work with a *madrich, madrichah,* or classmate to read the information aloud.
- Have the learner use an index card to track the line being read or to cover the portion of the page not being viewed. For example, in any of the "Reading Practice" activities the learner could cover the lines

that are not being read. Be willing to provide an alternative activity such as highlighting instead of circling key vocabulary.

For Learners with Dyslexia

- Enlarge the font. Don't be afraid to enlarge the content on a written page using a copier, if you do not have resources such as iPads or other devices that allow you to manipulate the size of the words on a page.
- Minimize other distractions on the page. You can create a "word viewer" of any size by cutting a word- or sentence-shaped hole in the center of a piece of card stock. Such a tool is most effective when customized to the individual learner. For example, ask the learner how much of the text he or she would prefer to be covered. Also ensure the size of the "viewer" is something the child has the dexterity to manipulate independently.
- Use color coding to distinguish vowel sounds and look-alike letters.
- Remove time limits. Learners with dyslexia feel anxious when they are expected to read at the pace of their peers. Allow learners to read at their own pace.

For Learners with Emotional Concerns

- Establish your classroom as a safe space for learning and building relationships by letting learners know that they are each valued and that everyone will be treated with kindness and respect.
- Provide positive reinforcement regularly to boost self-esteem and to encourage those who are shy to participate.
- Allow learners to participate in shared reading, if they prefer, rather than reading out loud individually.
- Allow learners to read one-on-one with the teacher or a *madrich/madrichah* until they feel more confident.
- Encourage positive relationships among learners by engaging in activities such as the ones listed above in "Foster Relationships among Learners." Ongoing mixers and get-to-know-you-type activities are very helpful for children who have emotional concerns. Other ways to foster relationships are to rearrange seats regularly and assign learners to work with different classmates each session.

For Learners Who Have Behavioral Challenges

- Establish positive relationships with the learner and his or her parents. Get to know the parents personally. Go out of your way to interact with them outside the classroom, if you can. Let parents know that you are always available to them to support their child. Offer multiple ways to contact you, and be responsive to parent communication.
- Set firm but reasonable expectations. Be clear with your classroom rules so learners know when they are not following them. Make it known to learners what is expected of them (*positive attitude, consistent attendance, trying their best, etc.*) and what they can expect of you, as their teacher (*treating all students fairly, being willing to give extra help, having a positive attitude, etc.*).
- Document what you see. Explaining what you see rather than your interpretation of what you feel happened is a more productive way to partner with administrators and/or parents to support the learner.
- Communicate with parents frequently; share the positive and strategize together to tackle the challenges their child is having in class.

- Find out what strategies work for the learner at home and in secular/day school to mirror in your own classroom where possible.
- Minimize transitions such as changing activities abruptly, and inform learners of schedule changes.

Remember that each learner is unique and will likely not fall entirely into any one category. All learners will benefit from a combination of various strategies.

USING *SHALOM HEBREW!*

The following are specific ways to use *Shalom Hebrew!* with learners of all abilities.

Teaching the key word

- Show a tangible object when introducing a key word. For example, bring in a *hanukkiyah* and candles when you teach the word *shamash* (lesson 2) or a tallit for lesson 15.
- Show the key word as it appears in other contexts. For example, together find the word *v'ahavta* (lesson 6) in your congregation's siddur.
- Where possible, connect a food item to the key word. For example, bring challah for the class to eat when you teach lesson 11.
- Connect the key word to a physical action. For example, in lesson 12, have learners "go up" to the *bimah* as you teach the key word *aliyah*.

Teaching New Letters and Vowels

- When you introduce a new letter or vowel, have the learners move their bodies into the shape of the letter while saying its sound. For example, when *resh* is introduced on page 17, have learners shape their bodies into *resh* while saying, "*Resh* says 'Rrrr.'"
- In addition to listening to and saying the name of new letters and the sounds of new vowels out loud, learners can shape letters out of bendable material such as pipe cleaners, Wikki Stix, or even clay.
- Learners can "draw" each letter in shaving cream or finger paint as they say its name and sound.

Doing the "Reading Practice" Activities

- Give learners index cards to track the line being read and to cover the portion of the page not being viewed. For example, in each "Reading Practice" activity, the learner can cover all the lines they are not reading.
- Be willing to offer an alternative activity such as highlighting instead of circling key words or vocabulary. For example, on page 8, in "Name Game," allow learners to highlight *shin, tav,* and *bet* instead of circling. Circling can be a complicated action for students with fine motor challenges.
- Have learners record themselves while reading so that they can go back and listen, checking for possible pronunciation errors.
- A variation of the activity above is to have two students record themselves and exchange recordings to check one another's reading. Students can review together any errors they have made and then rerecord themselves to correct those errors.

Completing Other Activities

- For "Read and Understand" (pages 29 and 48), ask students which words they know, in Hebrew and English, and have them join you in illustrating them, when possible. Display the pictures around the room. Add to the display throughout the year.

- Be willing to allow for an alternative activity such as highlighting instead of drawing a line from word to word. For example, on page 39 in "Word Link," allow learners to highlight each word as they read instead of drawing lines. Some students with fine motor challenges may have trouble drawing lines between words and may inadvertently cross words out in this activity.

- Create a "word viewer" for students to use as they complete various activities by cutting a word- or sentence-shaped hole in the middle of a large index card. This will help students focus on a specific word or sentence. For example, on page 42 in the "Making Meaning" activity, the word finder will enable students to focus on one vocabulary word at a time. It might also be helpful to copy the word bank of English definitions onto a separate page.

ASSESSMENT SHEETS
PLACEMENT TEST

Name_____ Date_____

	Lesson		Lesson		Lesson
26. אַפְקִיד	18	14. לְהָבִין	10	1. בַּת	1
27. לוֹחֵץ	19	15. נְשָׁמָה		2. שָׁת	
28. אֵילַת		16. מִנְחָה	11	3. בָּמֶה	2
29. עֲשֶׂרֶת	20	17. יַבָּשָׁה	12	4. לָמֶה	3
30. שְׂפָתַי		18. יָדַיִם	13	5. מַכָּה	
31. מָגֵן	21	19. מְאֹד	14	6. מָכְרָה	4
32. פּוֹתֵחַ		20. דָּתוֹ		7. הַבְרָה	5
33. מְשַׁבָּח	22	21. מִצְוֹת		8. דָּרְשָׁה	
34. פָּסוּק		22. בִּטָּחוֹן	15	9. וְאָכַל	6
35. מִזְמוֹר	23	23. שְׁמוֹנֶה	16	10. קָצַר	7
36. אוֹתְךָ	24	24. אֱמֶת		11. תִּקְוָה	8
37. יִמְלֹךְ		25. מְסַפֶּרֶת	17	12. שִׁירָה	
38. כָּתֵף	25			13. עֲתִיקָה	9

Comments: _____
_____
_____
_____

ASSESSMENT: Lessons 1–6

Name_____ Date_____

Lesson 6	Lesson 5	Lesson 4	Lesson 2-3	Lesson 1	
וָו	בַּד	בַּר	מַש	שָ	1.
לָו	שָב	מָכַר	מַבְ	תַ	2.
אָהַב	כָּתַב	לְכָה	לָה	בַּ	3.
אַתָּר	דְבַשׁ	כָּכָה	בַּמַשׁ	תָּ	4.
שָׁוְא	דָבָר	רָכַשׁ	מָשֵׁשׁ	תַּת	5.
רַאֲוָה	הָלָכָה	שָׁכַר	שָׁמָשׁ	שָׁת	6.
אָבְדָה	לָמְדָה	בְּכָתָה	מַכָּה	בַּת	7.
מִלְוָה	דְרָשָׁה	הָלַכְתְּ	מָשָׁל	בַּשָ	8.
אַדְוָה	הַבְרָה	כָּרַכְתְּ	כַּמָה	שַׁבַּת	9.
וְאָהַבְתָּ	הַבְדָלָה	בְּרָכָה	הַכַּלָה	שַׁבָּת	10.
Score					
Date					

ASSESSMENT: Lessons 7–13

Name_____ Date_____

	Lesson 7	Lesson 8-9	Lesson 10	Lesson 11	Lesson 12-13
1.	קַר	צַדִי	דָן	צַח	יָד
2.	צֵל	דַע	נָא	חַד	צָם
3.	קָהָל	אִשָּׁה	בְּנִי	שָׁכַח	יַעַר
4.	מָצָא	תִּיק	לָבָן	חֶבֶל	תְּרַם
5.	קָשַׁרְתְּ	שָׁמַע	נַעַר	חִכָּה	מַיִם
6.	צַוָּאר	אֲוִיר	מִשְׁנָה	חַלָּה	אָשָׁם
7.	מַמְתָּק	רָקִיעַ	נָבִיא	חֲמִשָּׁה	עֲלִיָּה
8.	צְדָקָה	שִׁבְעָה	כַּוָּנָה	בָּחַרְתָּ	קָמִים
9.	וְרָצָה	מִצְוָה	קַנְקַן	רַחֲמָן	אֲנָשִׁים
10.	בְּבַקָּשָׁה	תְּקִיעָה	נִשְׁתַּנָּה	שַׁחֲרִית	לְחַיִּים
Score					
Date					

ASSESSMENT: Lessons 14–19

Name_____ Date_____

	Lesson 14	Lesson 15	Lesson 16–17	Lesson 18	Lesson 19
1.	כֹּל	טַל	פֶּה	פִּי	שֵׁם
2.	יוֹם	קָט	סַל	אֶפֶס	עֵץ
3.	שָׁמַע	מָטָר	אֱמֶת	שֶׁפַע	מִיץ
4.	נָכוֹן	שְׁבָט	פֶּסַח	כֹּפֶר	פֶּרֶץ
5.	אָבוֹת	אָטָד	נֶאֱמָן	שׁוֹפָר	תּוֹקֵעַ
6.	יַעֲקֹב	טַלִּית	סַבְתָּא	פּוֹדֶה	אֱלֹהֵי
7.	תּוֹרָה	עֲטָרָה	לַעֲסֹק	צוֹפִיָה	חַסְדֵּי
8.	כֹּהֲנִים	נְטִילַת	נִכְנָס	טוֹטָפֶת	לִבְנֵי
9.	הַמּוֹצִיא	חֲטָאִים	מַסְפִּיק	תְּפִילִין	צָפוֹן
10.	מִצְווֹת	בִּטָּחוֹן	סְלִיחָה	נוֹפְלִים	נִצְטַוָּה
Score					
Date					

ASSESSMENT: Lessons 20–25

Name_____ Date_____

Lesson 25	Lesson 23–24	Lesson 22	Lesson 21	Lesson 20	
סַף	פָּז	הוּא	חַג	שָׁם	1.
דֶּרֶךְ	כַּף	צוּד	נֹחַ	שָׂק	2.
אָלֶף	לְךָ	סֻכָּה	גָּדֵל	שֵׂעָר	3.
פִּקֵּחַ	רֵעֶךָ	חֻמָשׁ	גֶּפֶן	תַּיִשׁ	4.
לְשַׁבֵּץ	מִזְבֵּחַ	בָּרְכוּ	עֶנֶג	שָׂשׂוֹן	5.
נִשְׂרַף	גָּזוּם	שֻׁלְחָן	פְּקֵחַ	עָשָׂה	6.
נָכוֹן	סוֹמֵךְ	קָדוּשׁ	הִשִּׂיג	פָּשַׁט	7.
צְבָעִים	מְבָרֵךְ	נְטוּיָה	מִשְׁלוֹחַ	עֲשֶׂרֶת	8.
כְּפוּפִים	וּבִשְׁעָרֶיךָ	וַיְנַסּוּ	הַצְלִיחַ	שִׂמְחַת	9.
לְהִתְעַטֵּף	מִצְוֹותֶיךָ	שָׁבוּעוֹת	אֶתְרוֹג	יִשְׂרָאֵל	10.
Score					
Date					

ANSWER KEYS

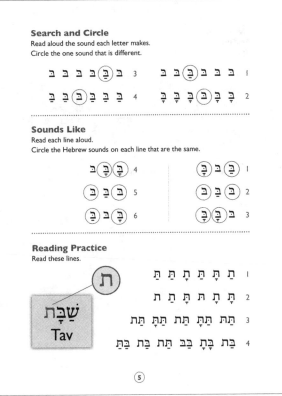

Word Find

Read the sounds on each game board with a classmate. Find and circle the word שַׁבָּת on each game board. Look across, down, and diagonally.

Name Game

Say the sound of each Hebrew letter. Then circle its name.

BET	(SHIN)	TAV	שׁ
(TAV)	BET	SHIN	ת
SHIN	TAV	(BET)	בּ
BET	(TAV)	SHIN	תּ

(8)

② שָׁמָשׁ
Shamash, Helper

מ

Sound the Symbols

Say the name and sound of each letter you have learned.
Then say the sound of each vowel.

שׁ ת תּ ב

◯ָ ◯ַ

Reading Practice

Read these lines.

שָׁמָשׁ
Mem

1 מ מַ מָ מַ מ מ

2 מַ ב ת תָ מָ שָׁ

3 מ מַ שׁ שַׁ מָ שׁ

4 בְּמָ מָשׁ בָּשׁ מַב

5 מַם שַׁב שָׁם מַשׁ

(9)

Reading Practice

Read aloud the word parts and words below.

1 שָׁם מָשׁ מַמָ מָשׁ שַׁב בָּת

2 מַשׁ מַב מָת מַם מַת מַבּ

3 בְּמַ שָׁמָ תָמָ בַּת בָּמָ תַם

4 מָשַׁב מְתָשׁ מַבַּת מַמַת בְּמָשׁ

5 תָמַשׁ שַׁבָּת תַמַת מַבַּשׁ מְשַׁשׁ

6 שַׁבָּת (שָׁמָשׁ) מָתָשׁ מָשָׁשׁ (שָׁמָשׁ)

7 שָׁם (שָׁמָשׁ) שַׁבּ שַׁבָּת (שָׁמָשׁ)

8 שַׁבָּת (שָׁמָשׁ) שַׁבָּת (שָׁמָשׁ) שַׁבָּת

Word Power

In the lines above, read and circle the Hebrew word for the helper candle on the *hanukkiyah*. How many words did you circle? 6
Describe one way a Hanukkah candle is similar to a שַׁבָּת candle and two ways it is different.
Similar:
1_____

Different:
1_____
2_____

(10)

Two of a Kind

On each line:
1 Say the sounds of the letters.
2 Circle the two identical letters.
3 Write the name of the letter you circled.

Shin	1 (שׁ) ב ת מ (שׁ)
Mem	2 שׁ (מ) ת (מ) ב
Tav	3 ב (תּ) מ (תּ) שׁ
Bet	4 מ (בּ) שׁ ת (בּ)
Tav	5 מ שׁ (ת) ב (ת)

Chunk It

Draw an arch over each syllable in the words below.

מָשׁ   בָּת   שַׁבָּת   שָׁמָשׁ

Now read the words to a partner.
Check off each word when you read it correctly.

Tic-Tac-Toe

Play tic-tac-toe with a friend.
Read the sounds correctly to mark an X or an O.

3			2			1		
תָ	בְּ	שָׁ	מָ	ב	ת	בַּ	שׁ	תַ
מ	ת	מָ	שָׁ	תַ	בְּ	שׁ	תָ	מ
שׁ	בַּ	תָ	שָׁ	מ	בּ	ת	מַ	ב

(11)

③

כַּלָה
Bride

(ה) (כ) (ל)

Sound the Symbols
Say the name and sound of each letter you have learned.
Then say the sound of each vowel.

ב ת ת שׁ מ

Reading Practice
Read these lines.

1 ל ל ל ל ל ל
2 מ מָ מ ל ל לָ
3 תָ שׁ מ ת בָ לָ
4 תַל לָמ לָשׁ לַשׁ לַב
5 מַל שָׁל לַת בַּל

כַּלָה
Lamed

⑫

Tongue Twisters
Take the challenge and read these tongue twisters aloud.

1 מַל מָל לַם לָל מַל מַמ
2 שַׁ בַּשׁ בַּל בַּל לַב בַּל שָׁב
3 לָשׁ שָׁת לַב לַת תָת
4 שָׁמָ תַּם שַׁב בַּת בָּמַ
5 מַל בָּל שָׁל תָמַ לָם

Reading Practice
Read these lines.

1 כ כַּ כָ כ כָ כַ
2 מַ שׁ ת ל בָ כַ
3 מ כַּ בָ ת כַ בָ
4 בַּ מַכ מָ כַּם כָּל
5 כַּת לַכ בַּכ כַּשׁ

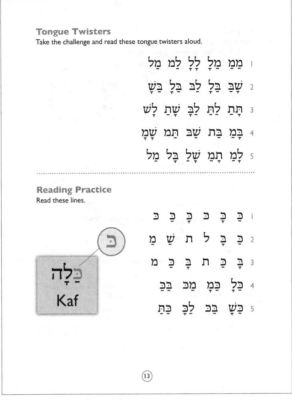

כַּלָה
Kaf

⑬

Search and Circle
Read aloud the Hebrew sounds on each line. Circle the Hebrew that sounds
the same as the English in the box. Say the name of the circled letter.

1 [LAH] בַ כ שׁ תַ (לַ) בַ
2 [M] ל כַ ת מָ (מ) מָ
3 [TAH] מ בַ מַ שׁ (תַ) בַ
4 [K] תַ בַ מ שׁ (כ) מ
5 [SHAH] מ בּ שׁ בַ (שׁ) מ

Reading Practice
Read these lines.

1 ה ה ה ה ה הָ
2 הַ שׁ מָ ל כַּ ה
3 הַת הַשׁ הַמ הַכ
4 שַׁב כַּל הַב הַשׁ

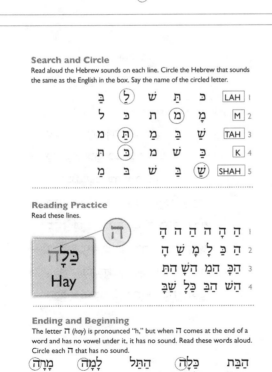

כַּלָה
Hay

Ending and Beginning
The letter ה (hay) is pronounced "h," but when ה comes at the end of a
word and has no vowel under it, it has no sound. Read these words aloud.
Circle each ה that has no sound.

מָרָ(ה) לָ(מָה) הַתַּל כַּלָ(ה) הַבַּ(ת)

ה at the beginning of a word often means "the." הַשַׁבָּת means "the
Shabbat." *CHALLENGE:* What does הַשַׁמָשׁ mean? _the shamash,
the helper_

⑭

Reading Practice
Read aloud the word parts and words below.

1 הָ כַּ הָ תָ הָ בַּ
2 הַה הָת הָשׁ הַת הָב הַל
3 הַה מַה לָה שֵׁה תָה בָּה
4 שַׁבָּת כַּמָה לָשָׁה בָּמָה תָלָה
5 לָשָׁה כַּלָה שָׁמָה מַכָּה לָמָה
6 הַכַּלָה הַמְשָׁל הַשַׁבָּת הַשֶׁמֶשׁ הַבַּת
7 לָשָׁה לָמָה כַּמָה מַכָּה הַכַּלָה כַּלָה
8 (שַׁבָּת הַכַּלָה) (שַׁבָּת הַכַּלָה) (שַׁבָּת הַכַּלָה)

Word Power
Read and circle the Hebrew phrase above for the Shabbat bride,
שַׁבָּת הַכַּלָה. How many times did you read the phrase for the
Shabbat bride? __3__

Think about it: In what ways is Shabbat like a bride?

⑮

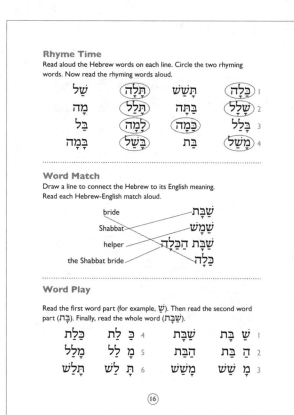

Rhyme Time

Read aloud the Hebrew words on each line. Circle the two rhyming words. Now read the rhyming words aloud.

שֶׁל	(תְּלָה)	תְּשֵׁשׁ	(כְּלָה) 1
מָה	(תְּלָל)	בַּתָּה	(שְׁלָל) 2
בֵּל	(לְמָה)	(כְּמָה)	בְּלָל 3
בְּמָה	(בְּשָׁל)	בַּת	(מְשָׁל) 4

Word Match

Draw a line to connect the Hebrew to its English meaning. Read each Hebrew-English match aloud.

bride — שַׁבָּת
Shabbat — שֶׁמֶשׁ
helper — שַׁבָּת הַכַּלָּה
the Shabbat bride — כַּלָּה

Word Play

Read the first word part (for example, שַׁ). Then read the second word part (בָּת). Finally, read the whole word (שַׁבָּת).

כַּלַּת	כַּ לַת	4	שַׁבָּת	שַׁ בָּת	1
מְלָל	מָ לַל	5	הַבַּת	הַ בַּת	2
תְּלָשׁ	תָּ לַשׁ	6	מְשָׁשׁ	מְ שָׁשׁ	3

16

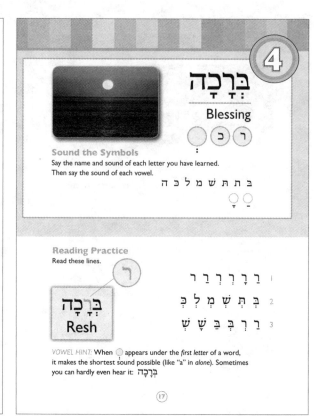

④

בְּרָכָה

Blessing

ר כ ◯
:

Sound the Symbols

Say the name and sound of each letter you have learned. Then say the sound of each vowel.

ב ת שׁ ת מ ל כ ה
◯ ◯
ָ

Reading Practice

Read these lines.

ר

בְּרָכָה
Resh

רַ רָ רְ רִ רִ ר	1
בְּ תְ שְׁ מְ לְ כְּ	2
רַ רְ בְּ שֵׁ שִׁ	3

VOWEL HINT: When ◯ appears under the *first letter* of a word, it makes the shortest sound possible (like "a" in *alone*). Sometimes you can hardly even hear it: בְּרָכָה

17

Name Tag

Circle the name of each Hebrew letter. What sound does each letter make?

HAY	(TAV)	SHIN	ת 1
SHIN	KAF	(BET)	ב 2
(RESH)	HAY	TAV	ר 3
HAY	(SHIN)	BET	שׁ 4
KAF	(HAY)	TAV	ה 5
MEM	SHIN	(LAMED)	ל 6
LAMED	(KAF)	BET	כ 7
(MEM)	LAMED	TAV	מ 8

Reading Practice

Read these lines.

בְּרָכָה
Chaf

כַ כָ כִ כ כָ כְ	1
כַּ בָּ כִּ כָּ כָּ כָ	2
כְ כִּ בָּ כ כ בּ	3
בְּכַ לַכַּ כָה כִּ	4

18

VOWEL HINT: When ◯ appears in the *middle* of a word, it usually makes no sound. *It stops the syllable:* מַלְכָּה

Reading Practice

Read aloud the word parts and words below.

מָכַ בְּכַ כְּכָ רַכ תָּכ לְכָ	1
כָה מָכַ כְּכָ כִב כַּת כֵשׁ	2
רַכ כָּמ שַׁכ כַּר תַכ בַּר	3
בְּכָה כְּכָה רַכָה מָכַר שָׁכַר כַּלַת	4
כַּלָּה כָּהָה כַּמָה מַכָּה רָכַשׁ לַכַת	5
בְּכַת כָכַת כְּרָה לְכָה תָּכָה לָכַשׁ	6
בְּכְתָה הַתָּכָה כָּרַכְתְּ מְכְרָה הָלַכְתְּ	7
הָלַכְתְּ (בְּרָכָה) (בְּרָכָה) הָלְכָה מָשְׁכָה	8

19

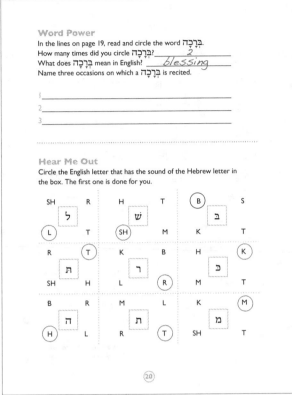

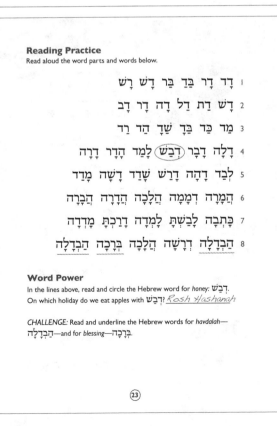

Word Find

Read all the sounds on each game board. Find and circle the word that appears above each game board. Look from right to left, up and down, and diagonally.

3 שַׁבָּת   2 הַבְדָלָה   1 בְּרָכָה

Sounds Like

Circle the Hebrew sound on each line that is the same as the Hebrew in the box.

הַר	(הַב)	תַב	הַב 1
בֵּר	(בַּד)	בַּד	בַּד 2
(רֵשׁ)	רָתָה	דְשָׁה	רֵשׁ 3
כַּב	בַּב	(כַּךְ)	כַּךְ 4
(דַבֵּר)	רָבָד	דָבַה	דָבֵּר 5
בָּלָה	(בַּל)	כַּלָה	בָּלָה 6

Word Play

Read the first word part (for example, שֶׁ).
Then read the second word part (בַל).
Finally, read the whole word (שֶׁבַל).

תָּהָה	תָּ הָה	7	שֶׁבַל	שֶׁ בַל	1
הַכְּבָּרָה	הַכְ בָּרָה	8	כָּלָה	כָּ לָה	2
דָּבָר	דָּ בָר	9	שֶׁבְרָה	שֶׁבְ רָה	3
בְּרָכָה	בְּךְ כָה	10	לָמְדָה	לָמְ דָה	4
רָכֶשְׁתְּ	רָ כֶשְׁתְּ	11	בְּכְתָה	בְּךְ תָה	5
מָרֵר	מָ רֵר	12	רָמָה	רָ מָה	6

Move It and Use It

Read each Hebrew word below. Then write or draw the English meaning on the line below the word.

שַׁמָשׁ	כַּלָה	שַׁבָּת	דְבַשׁ
shamash, helper	bride	Shabbat	honey

בְּרָכָה	הַבְדָלָה	מַלְכָּה
blessing	Havdalah separation	queen

CHALLENGE: Can you use each Hebrew word in an English sentence? Example: We welcome שַׁבָּת by lighting candles.

6
וְאָהַבְתָּ
You Shall Love

ר   ו   א

Sound the Symbols

Say the name and sound of each letter you have learned.
Then say the sound of each vowel.

ב ת שׁ מ ל כ כ ה ה ר כ ב ד

◌ֻ ◌ָ ◌ֲ ◌ַ

Reading Practice

Read these lines.

וְאָהַבְתָּ
Alef

אַ אֶ אֶ אַ אַ אַ	1
אַ שֶׁ לִ הַ רָ בְ	2
אַ הַ אַ דָ כְ רְ	3
אַת לָ בָּא אַב	4
בָּאָה רָאָה אָמַר שָׁאַל	5

Reading Practice

Read these lines.

וְאָהַבְתָּ
Vav

וְ וַ וְ וִ וֹ וֻ	1
אֶ דְ בָ רְ כֶ הַ	2
וְ וַ בְ בַ רְ ד	3

Chunk It

Draw an arch over each syllable in the words below.

בְּרָא   אָמְרָה   אַבָּא   הַבְדָלָה   כַּלָה

אָכְלָה   אָדָר   אַתָּה   אֲדָמָה   אָבְדָה

Now read the words to a partner. Check off each word when you read it correctly.

Word Match

Draw a line to match the Hebrew to its English meaning.
Read each Hebrew-English match aloud.

Shabbat	בְּרָכָה 1
blessing	וְאָהַבְתָּ 2
you shall love	שַׁבָּת 3
havdalah, separation	כַּלָה 4
helper	הַבְדָלָה 5
bride	שַׁמָשׁ 6

Reading Practice
Read aloud the word parts and words below.

1   דָו שָו תָו שְו וָל וְה

2   וָו וָה וַת וַר וַד וָא

3   לָו מָו כְו הָו תָו בֻּו

4   דָור שָוֶה תָוֶה אָוֶה לָו אָבָה

5   אַתָר דָוֶה הָוֶה שָוְא וָלָד דְבַשׁ

6   אַשָרָה אַדְוָה רַאֲוָה וְאַתָּה וְאָהַב

7   אָבְדָה שַׁלְוָה וְאָכַל מִלְוָה הַדָבָר

8   וְהָלַכְתָ (וְאָהַבְתָ) וְאָמַרְתָ וְלָמַדְתָ (וְאָהַבְתָ)

Word Power
The Hebrew word וְאָהַבְתָ (you shall love) is the first word of one of our most important prayers. The וְאָהַבְתָ tells us to love God. Find and circle וְאָהַבְתָ above.

What do you think it means to love God?

_____

_____

(28)

Read and Understand
You already know the meaning of some of these Hebrew words. Read all the words aloud. Put a check next to words that are familiar.
CHALLENGE: Pick two new words to read and understand.

בַּת daughter	תָּמָר date	מַר Mr.	שָׁר sings	בֵּר son
רַב rabbi	שַׁבָּת Shabbat	רַבַּת many	שָׁת put	דָת religion
שָׁמַר guarded	שָׁבַר broke	דָבָר thing	שָׁב returned	בַּד linen
בָּרָד hail	מָשָׁל proverb	לָמַד studied	לָבַשׁ wore	שַׁמָשׁ helper
בְּרָכָה blessing	כַּלָה bride	דְבַשׁ honey	הַבְדָלָה separation	דָרַשׁ explained
לָמָה why	מַלְכָּה queen	וָו hook	רָאֲתָה she saw	בָּכָה cried

Silent Partner
Cross out the letter in each pair that makes no sound.
Write the sound of the other letter.

1   ב אֶ _v_ 10   שׁ אֶ _sh_ 7   אֶ ת _t_ 4   ב אֶ _b_ 1

2   ד אֶ _d_ 11   אֶ ל _l_ 8   כָּ אֶ _k_ 5   מ אֶ _m_ 2

3   כ אֶ _ch_ 12   אֶ ה _h_ 9   אֶ ר _r_ 6   ת אֶ _t_ 3

(29)

---

⑦

צְדָקָה

Justice

ק   צ

Sound the Symbols
Say the name and sound of each letter you have learned.
Then say the sound of each vowel.

ב ת ת שׁ מ ל כ ה ר כ ב

ד א וּ

◯ ◯ ◯ ◯
ָ ׃ ׃ ָ

Reading Practice
Read these lines.

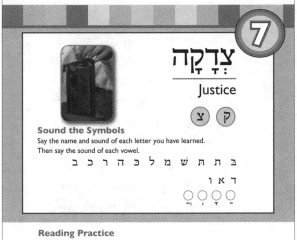

צְדָקָה
Koof

1   ק ק ק ק ק ק

2   ק ר ק ק כְ וֹ

3   ק כְ כ כֹ הָ אָ

4   קַו רַק קָר בַּק

5   קְרָב רָקַד דָקָה שֶׁקֶל

(30)

Reading Practice
Read these lines.

צ

צְדָקָה
Tzadee

1   צ צ צַ צְ צָ צָ

2   ק צַ כֹ קָ צָ ל

3   צַ ק צַ קָ כָ ד

4   צַר רָצַ וְק בַּק

5   קָשַׁר קָצַר בְּצַד רָצְתָ

Move It and Use It
In modern Hebrew וְ at the beginning of a word means "and." Draw a קַו (line) from each Hebrew phrase to its matching picture(s). Look to see if there is רַק (only) one item or if there is one item וְ (and) a second item.

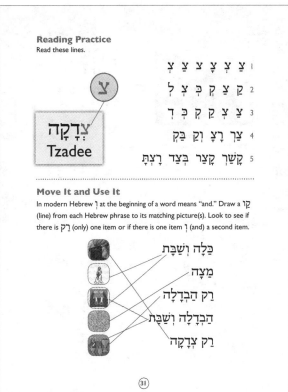

כַּלָה וְשַׁבָּת

מַצָה

רַק הַבְדָלָה

הַבְדָלָה וְשַׁבָּת

רַק צְדָקָה

(31)

Reading Practice
Read aloud the word parts and words below.

צַו עָב צַר צַד צָה עָל ₁

כְּצ בָּצ אָצ מַצ קְצ רָצ ₂

אָכָה צָדַק כְּצַד בָּצַר אָצָה צָרָה ₃

צָבָא צָבַּר קָצַר צְבָת בָּצַל מָצָא ₄

מַצָה קְצַת קַצָב מַצָב הַצָב אָצַר ₅

מָצָא צָלָה צָמַד מַצָה אָצְתָ צָמָא ₆

וְרָצָה וְאָצַר צָרַמְתְּ צַוָאר צָוָאה ₇

צְדָקָה בְּצָרַת מָצָאתָ צָדַקְתָ צְדָקָה ₈

Word Power
Can you find these Hebrew words above? Circle, then read them.

justice צְדָקָה   matzah מַצָה

The word צְדָקָה is also used for giving to those in need.
What is a connection between justice and giving to those in need?

(32)

Stop and Go
With a partner, read all of the words aloud. At the beginning of a word,
◌ always makes a short "UH" sound. It lets you GO. See the example in
the box on line 1.
Sometimes ◌ has no sound. It tells you to STOP. See the circled
example on line 2. Put a box around the words in which ◌ makes a
short "UH" sound. Circle the words in which ◌ tells you to stop.

Sound Off
Say the name of the Hebrew letter in each box. Circle the English letter
that makes the same sound as the Hebrew letter.

(33)

מִצְוָה (8)
Commandment

Sound the Symbols
Say the name and sound of each letter you have learned.
Then say the sound of each vowel.

ב כ ר ה ה כ ל מ שׁ ת ת ב
ד א ו ק צ

◌ ◌ ◌ ◌

Reading Practice
Read these lines.

א ו ה מ ת בּ ₁

צ לִי כִּי רַ כַ דִי ₂

אִי בִּי כִּי לִי מִי וִי ₃

לִיק הִיא רְמָ דִיל ₄

צִיל דַבּ מִרְמָ מִקֵן בְּקֵן ₅

(34)

Reading Practice
Read aloud the word parts and words below.

מִק צַדִי לִבִי אֲוִי דֵו בְּרִי ₁

שָׁשָׁה הִכָּה בִּיב שְׁמִי צִיר הַכִי ₂

הִיא אִישׁ אִשָׁה אִמָא בְּכִי בְּלִי ₃

רַבִּי אֲוִיר דָוִד בִּימָה דָתִי תִּיק ₄

שִׁירָה תִּירָא רָמָה קְרִיאָה לִבִיבָה קָצִיר ₅

צַדִיק בְּרִיאַת קַדִישׁ אָבִיב קְהִילָה מִקְרָא ₆

צִיצִית בְּרִית מִילָה תִּקְנָה הַתִּקְוָה ₇

מִצְוָה הַמִצְוָה בַּר מִצְוָה בַּת מִצְוָה ₈

Word Power
Can you find these Hebrew words above? Circle, then read them.

knotted fringes	צִיצִית	bar mitzvah	בַּר מִצְוָה
commandment	מִצְוָה	bat mitzvah	בַּת מִצְוָה
Kaddish	קַדִישׁ	the Hope,	
		Israel's national anthem	הַתִּקְוָה

A בַּת מִצְוָה or בַּר מִצְוָה often wears a tallit. The tallit has knotted
fringes on its four corners.

(35)

Move It and Use It

קְדִימָה Stand and read each of the following words aloud. Take a step (forward) when you read a word correctly.

1 מַצָה לְבִיבָה בִּימָה צִיצִית
2 מְדַבֵּר דְבַשׁ צְדָקָה לְהַדְלִיק
3 מִצְוָה אִשָּׁה מַצִיל אָבִיו

Draw a קַו (line) under the food we eat on Passover.

Dalet-Resh Race

Take turns reading the lines. Watch out for the look-alike letters!

1 ד דִי דָ ד דִי דִ דָ ד
2 רַ רָ ר רִי רִ רָ רִי רַ
3 דָק רִיב רָב דִית רַד
4 דָר קָרָא תָּמִיד מִדְרָשׁ

Put It Together

Choose a partner. Together or one at a time, read the word parts and then the whole words in the boxes below.

4	3	2	1
הַתִק זָה	דָב רָה	מִצ וָה	מַב דִיל
הַתִּקְוָה	דִבְרָה	מִצְוָה	מַבְדִיל
הַתִּקְנָה	דִבְרָה	מִצְנָה	מַבְדִיל

(36)

שְׁמַע
Hear

ע

Sound the Symbols

Say the name and sound of each letter you have learned. Then say the sound of each vowel.

ב כ ר ה כ ל מ שׁ ת ת ב
ד א ו ק צ

◯ ◯ ◯ ◯ ◯ ◯ יִ

Reading Practice

Read these lines.

1 עָ עִי עַ עָ עַ עָ
2 הָ אַ עַ הַ אַ עַ
3 עַ הָ אַ קִי אַ צִי עִי
4 בַּע מַע עב עָשׁ עָב
5 עָלָה עִיר אֶת קֶעָר צֶע

שְׁמַע
Ayin

(37)

Reading Practice

Read aloud the word parts and words below.

1 דַע מַע צָעִי עָב עָתִי עָשִׂי
2 עָר עִיר רַע עַד עָב עַל
3 עָבַר בַּעַל רַעַשׁ עַתָּה דַעַת וַעַד
4 שָׁעָה עִמָה תָּקַע צָעִיר רָעָב (שְׁמַע)
5 עִבְרִי עָתִיק אַרְבַּע עָשִׁיר עָתִיד רָקִיעַ
6 קְעָרָה (עֲמִידָה) תְּקִיעָה מַעֲרִיב עִבְרִית
7 (עֲמִידָה) עַתִיקָה שִׁבְעָה עָבַדְתִּי שָׁעוֹן
8 שְׁמַע קְרִיאַת שְׁמִיעָה תִּשְׁמַע (שְׁמַע)

Word Power

In the lines above, find and circle the names of two important prayers, the שְׁמַע and the עֲמִידָה. Why do you think it is traditional to cover our eyes when we say the שְׁמַע and to stand when we say the עֲמִידָה?

CHALLENGE: This year you are learning to read עִבְרִית (Hebrew). Can you find and underline this word above?

(38)

Checkout Line

Put a ✓ on each line where the two word parts sound the same. Put an X on the line if they sound different.

1 עִי עָ ✓   2 צָ עַ X   3 עַ עָ ✓   4 אִי קָ כִּי ✓
5 רָ וָ X   6 צָ אַ X   7 דִי ר X   8 אַ עָ ✓

Word Link

Read the words to a partner. Draw a line from word to word as you read each one correctly.

1 קָצִיר הַתִּקְוָה קַדִישׁ לָמַד מְכַרְתָּ
2 אִשָּׁה לָבַשׁ מִילָה רַבִּי שִׁירָה
3 צַדִיק דַעַת עָתִיד צִיצִית מָשָׁל

Word Play

Form a group of three. The first person reads the first word part (עַר). The second person reads the second word part (בָה). The third person reads the whole word (עַרְבָה). Continue in that way.

1 לְהַרְעִישׁ עִישׁ לְהַר 4   עַרְבָה בָה עַר
2 תְּקִיעָה עָה תְּקִי 5   לְמַעְלָה לָה לְמַע
3 בְּקִרְבִּי בִּי בְּקֶר 6   מַלְבִּישׁ בִּישׁ מַל

(39)

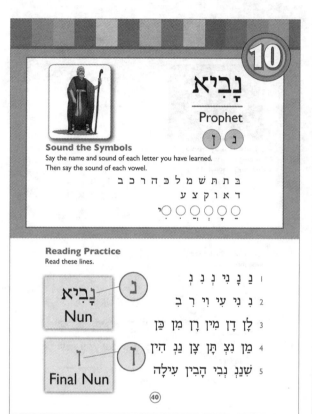

10

נָבִיא

Prophet

ן   נ

Sound the Symbols
Say the name and sound of each letter you have learned.
Then say the sound of each vowel.

ב כ ר ה כ ל מ שׁ ת ת ב
ע ק צ ו א ד

◯ֵ ◯ִ ◯ָ ◯ֶ ◯ַ ◯ִי

Reading Practice
Read these lines.

נ
נָבִיא
Nun

ן
Final Nun

1 נַ נָ נִי נְ נֵ נֹ

2 נָ נִי עִי וִי רְ בְ

3 לָן דָן מִין רָן מִן כֵּן

4 מַן נְצ תָן צָן נֵ הִין

5 שַׁנֵּ נְבִי הָבִין עִילָה

(40)

Reading Practice
Read aloud the word parts and words below.

1 נָן נָו נְעִי קָן בֵּין

2 נִין לָן דָן מָן שִׁין רָן

3 דִין בְּנִי עָנִי נָקִי אֲנִי נָא

4 שָׁנָה לָבָן עָנָו רִנָּה עָנֵד נַער

5 (נָבִיא) בִּינָה נְשָׁמָה מִשְׁנָה נְעָרָה

6 מַאֲמִין שְׁכִינָה כַּוָּנָה נְעִילָה מַרְבִּין

7 רַעֲנָן מִשְׁכָּן לְהָבִין קַנְקָן לַמְדָן

8 (נָבִיא) מְדִינָה (מָה) (נִשְׁתַּנָּה) (נָבִיא)

Word Power
Find and circle this Hebrew word above: נָבִיא (prophet).

CHALLENGE: At the Passover seder, the youngest child asks the Four
Questions. Find and circle the two Hebrew words in the lines above that
introduce the Four Questions. Now read all the circled words.

(41)

Move It and Use It
Read the words aloud.
1 Put a קַו (line) under the name of a character in the Purim story.
2 Put a square around the word for the platform in the synagogue where
we read the Torah.
3 Circle the word for gragger. *Hint:* It is built on the root letters רעשׁ (noise).
4 The colors of the Israeli flag are כָּחוֹל וְלָבָן (blue and white). Draw an
Israeli flag above the word for *white* below.

1 (רַעֲשָׁן)   צְעִירָה   לְהָבִין   צָבַּר   אַבְדָּה

2 קְרָא   לָמַד   🇮🇱לָבָן   עָבְדָה   הָמָן

3 בִּימָה   מְעִיל   מָשָׁל   לְמַעֲלָה   כָּתַב

Making Meaning
Write the English meaning below each of the Hebrew words or word parts.

prophet	helper	separation	and	Shabbat
blessing	bride	hear	justice	commandment

5 שֶׁמֶשׁ   4 כַּלָּה   3 צְדָקָה   2 שַׁבָּת   1 נָבִיא
helper   *bride*   *justice*   *Shabbat*   *prophet*

10 שְׁמַע   9 בְּרָכָה   8 וְ-   7 מִצְוָה   6 הַבְדָּלָה
hear   *blessing*   *and*   *commandment* *separation*

(42)

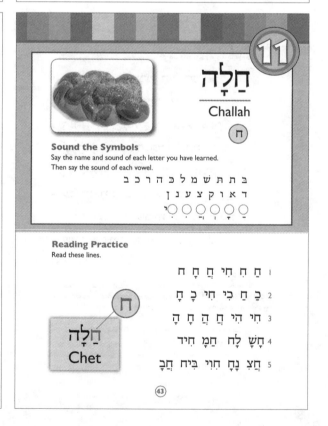

11

חַלָּה

Challah

ח

Sound the Symbols
Say the name and sound of each letter you have learned.
Then say the sound of each vowel.

ב כ ר ה כ ל מ שׁ ת ת ב
ן ע צ ק ו א ד

◯ִי ◯ַ ◯ֶ ◯ִ ◯ָ ◯ֵ

Reading Practice
Read these lines.

חַלָּה
Chet

ח

1 חַ חָ חִי חַ חָ חָ

2 כָּ חַ כִּי חִי כָ חָ

3 חִי הִי חַ הֵ חָ הָ

4 חָשׁ לָח חַם חִיד

5 חָא נָא חִוִי בִּיח חַב

(43)

Reading Practice

Read aloud the word parts and words below.

1 חַךְ חָבִי חָתָ בָּח אַח צָח

2 חָל חִיל חַד חָש חִיש חִימִי

3 קַח צַח נָח לָח אָח חַוָּה

4 חִבָּה שָׁכַח חָבִיב חֶבָל חָתָן לָקַח

5 חַלָּה חָלִיל וְצָחַק אַחַת חָצִיר חָנָן

6 מִנְחָה חֲמִישָׁה שְׁלָחָה חִירִיק בָּחַרְתָּ

7 רַחֲמָן הָרַחֲמָן שַׁחֲרִית חֲתִימָה חֲדָשָׁה

8 הַחַלָּה הַבְּרָכָה חַלָּה לְשַׁבָּת הָרַחֲמָן

Word Power

Can you find these Hebrew words above? Circle, then read them.

the Merciful One (God) הָרַחֲמָן   braided bread חַלָּה

CHALLENGE: Find the Hebrew word for *the blessing.*
Draw a קַו (line) under the word.

(44)

Hebrew Marathon

Watch out for the look-alike letters as you read each line.

1 חָ ח הִי הָ ה תָ תִי ת תַ

2 הֵא לַת מָה כָּה חִי בָּה בַּת

3 תָּה חַת רָה רָתָ חָה חִיל הַח

4 חַלָה תַּחַת לָקַחַת לְהַדְלִיק חָתָן

5 אַהֲבַת לְהַתְחִיל שַׁחֲרִית חַוָה בְּרִית

Sounds Like

Draw a קַו (line) to connect each letter/vowel combination that sounds the same.

עַ   בְּ   בְּ   תִי   חֶ

וִי   אָ   כָ   קָ   תַ

Baseball Rounds

With a partner, read a column of words to get on base. Read all three columns to score a home run.

Third Base	Second Base	First Base	
מַדְרִיכָה	עַרְבִית	בְּאַהֲבָה	1
שָׁכַח	חָבִיב	לְהַחְבִּיא	2
מִשְׁכָּן	שְׁכִינָה	כַּמָּה	3
בַּעַל	כַּוָּנָה	קַבְּלַת	4

(45)

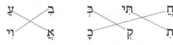

עֲלִיָּה
Going Up

ר

Sound the Symbols

Say the name and sound of each letter you have learned.
Then say the sound of each vowel.

ב ת ת ש מ ל כ ה ר ח כ ב
ד א ו ק צ ע נ נ ח

◌ ◌ ◌ ◌ ◌ ◌ י

Reading Practice

Read these lines.

1 רַ רָ רִי רִ רִי רְ

2 יַ וַ רָ וְ רִי וִי

3 יָשׁ יָר יָן יְשִׁי חַי יְדִי

4 יַבְ יָשׁ יִקְ יַח יָהִי יַל

5 יָשָׁן יָשָׁב יָשִׁי יָשִׁי יָקָר נִיָה

עֲלִיָּה
Yud

(46)

Reading Practice

Read the words below.

1 יָד יְהִי יַיִן יָמַי יָדַי יָמָה

2 שַׁיִשׁ יָשָׁן מִיָד נִיָר לַיִל הֱיִי

3 בַּיִת יָשָׁר יַעַר חַיָה עַיִן יָשַׁב

4 יָדַע אַיִל חַיָב יָחִיד יָקָר מַעְיָן

5 יְצִיר הָיָה יַיִן חַיִל יָצָא עֲדַיִן

6 יַחְדָו יִרְאָה יִצְחָק יַבָּשָׁה צִיַרְתִּי

7 עֲלִיָּה כְּוִיָה יוֹכַח יַלְדָה יְדִיעָה

8 יְשִׁיבָה יִשְׁתַּבַּח הָיְתָה מִנְיָן עֲלִיָּה

Word Power

Can you find these Hebrew words above? Circle, then read them.

aliyah, going up עֲלִיָּה
ten Jewish adults needed for a prayer service מִנְיָן

CHALLENGE: Use the words עֲלִיָּה and מִנְיָן in English sentences.

(47)

Reading Rules

When ◯ and ◯ are followed by the letter י at the end of a word, say "EYE" as in shy (שַׁי).

חַי דַי סִינַי מָתַי בְּחַיַי

When ◯י comes at the end of a word, the letter י is silent.

דְּבָרָיו רַחֲמָיו עַכְשָׁיו עָלָיו נְעָרָיו

Yud Marathon

Take turns reading these lines.

1 אִי חִיל כִּי מִיָּה
2 לִי יָד יְהִי יָדִי חַיִי
3 יָחִיד יָמָה יָרְדָה וַיְהִי יִצְחָק וַיְכַל
4 יַחַד יָצָא יָדְעָה יָדִית יְדִיד יָהִיר

Read and Understand

Read all the words aloud. Put a check next to those that are familiar to you.

יָרַד descended	יָשָׁר honest	עַל-יָד next to	יָרַשׁ inherited	עַיִן eye
שָׁמַע hear	יָד hand	דַיָּן judge	יָמִינָה to the right	תַּיָּר tourist
מַדְרִיכָה counselor	אֲבָל but	יַיִן wine	לְהַצְבִּיעַ to point	לָדַעַת to know
חָדָשׁ new	שָׁעָה hour	מְדִינָה state	שָׁאַל asked	נְיָר paper

48

13

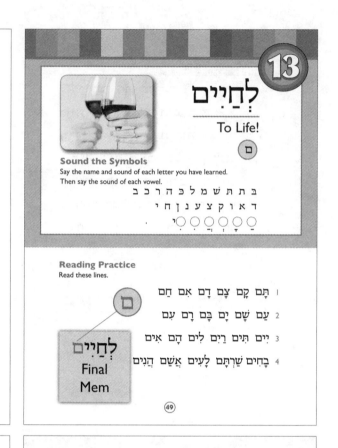

לְחַיִּים

To Life!

ם

Sound the Symbols

Say the name and sound of each letter you have learned.
Then say the sound of each vowel.

ב ת ת שׁ מ ל כ ה ר כ ב
ד א ו ק צ ע נ ן ח י
◯ִי ◯ ◯ ◯ ◯ ◯

Reading Practice

Read these lines.

1 תָּם קָם צָם דָּם אָם חַם
2 עַם שָׁם יָם בָּם רָם עִם
3 יָם תִּם רַיִם לִים הָם אִים
4 בָּחִים שַׁרְתָּם לָעִים אֲשֶׁם הֵנִים

לְחַיִּים
Final Mem

49

Reading Practice

Read the words below.

1 הָלַם אַחִים עָלִים מִרְיָם בַּדִּים תָּרֶם
2 אִים שָׁנַיִם בָּתִּים אָדָם דַּקִּים מִצְרַיִם
3 חָכָם רַעַם יָמִים רַבִּים חַיִּים דָּמָם
4 (בָּנִים) מַיִם אָדָם שְׁתַּיִם מִלִּים אָשָׁם
5 נָשִׁים שָׁמַיִם דְּבָרִים יָדַיִם קָמִים עָלִים
6 אַבְרָהָם נְבִיאִים כְּרָמִים שִׁבְעִים אֲנָשִׁים
7 עִבְרִים רַחֲמִים יְלָדִים צַדִּיקִים מְלָכִים
8 עֲבָדִים (יְצִיאַת מִצְרַיִם) (לְחַיִּים) (לְחַיִּים)

Word Power

Can you find these Hebrew words above? Circle, then read them.

boys, sons בָּנִים   לְחַיִּים to life
the Exodus, going out from Egypt יְצִיאַת מִצְרַיִם

CHALLENGE: How many בָּנִים are in your class? ____

50

Chet Tav Stretch

Stretch across. Read lines 1 through 4.
Stretch down. Read columns A through D.

D	C	B	A
חַיִּים	תִּרְצַח	תַּעֲנִי	חַלָּה
חָבַק	חֶבֶל	תַּחַת	חָבַב
הַחְרָשָׁה	תִּשְׁבִּי	צָרַחְתְּ	צַחֲקָה
תִּשְׁמַע	קָרָאתְ	לַחֵן	אַחֲרָיו

Rhyme Time

Read aloud the Hebrew words on each line. Circle the two rhyming words. Now read the rhyming words aloud.

1 מַיִם (כְּרִישׁ) קָנָה (קָדִישׁ)
2 (כַּוָּנָה) בְּרִית (מַתָּנָה) הָרַחֲמָן
3 הַמִּינִים (עָלָה) (כַּלָּה)✓ עִם
4 (צַיָּר) (צְדָקָה) שָׁם (תַּיָּר)
5 דָּן (מָן) דַּיָּן (דִּין)

CHALLENGE:
1. In "Rhyme Time," circle the word for *justice* or *helping those in need.*
2. Put a check ✓ above the word for *bride.*

51

Loud and Louder

When ◯ appears in the middle of a word, it usually ends a syllable and has no sound.
When ◯ appears under the first letter in a word it makes a short "UH" sound.
Read the lines below with a partner. Read the first word softly, then read the next words louder and louder.

1 הַבְדָלָה דִּבְּרַתָ מִצְוָה נִשְׁמָתִי שְׁבָרִים
2 עִבְרִית מִנְיָן בְּרָכָה נְבִיאִים וְקָים
3 מִשְׁכָּן דְּבָרִים לַחְמִי שְׁמִי אַבְרָהָם
4 תְּהִלָּה מִרְיָם קְצָת בִּנְיָמִן יְלָדִים

Making Meaning

Read aloud the Hebrew words in each line. Circle the word that has the same meaning as the English in the box.

1 שַׁמָּשׁ הַבְדָלָה חַלָּה (בְּרָכָה) | blessing
2 (לְחַיִּים) עֲבָדִים חָכָם מִצְוָה | to life
3 שְׁתַּיִם (שְׁמַע) בָּנִים נָבִיא | hear
4 יְצִיאַת עַיִן (עֲלִיָּה) מִצְרַיִם | going up
5 יְשִׁיבָה שָׁמַיִם (צְדָקָה) יְלָדִים | justice

(52)

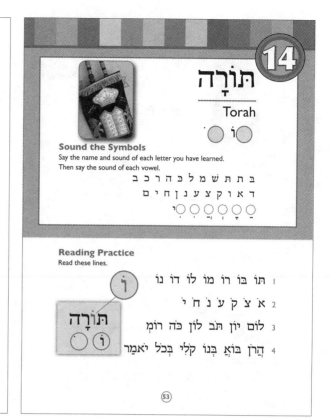

14
תּוֹרָה
Torah

Sound the Symbols

Say the name and sound of each letter you have learned.
Then say the sound of each vowel.

ב ת תּ שׁ מ ל כ ה ר ח כ ב
ד א ו ק צ ע נ ן ח י ם
◯ ◯ ◯ ◯ ◯ י

Reading Practice

Read these lines.

1 תּוֹ בּוֹ רוֹ מוֹ לוֹ דוֹ נוֹ
2 א צ ק ע נ ח ﬠ י
3 לוֹם יוֹן תֹּב לוֹן כֹּה רוֹם
4 הֲרָן בּוֹאֲ בְּנוֹ קְלִי בְּכָל יֹאמַר

(53)

Reading Practice

Read the words below.

1 כָּל [לֹא] אוֹת יוֹם חוֹל צֹאן
2 עוֹד קוֹל מוֹת שׁוֹר צוֹם חוֹר
3 שְׁמַע יָבֹא אַתֶּם דָתוֹ אָנֹכִי כְּמוֹ
4 אָבוֹת מְאֹד כְּבוֹד לָשׁוֹן שָׁעוֹת
5 קָדוֹשׁ (תּוֹרָה) צִיּוֹן (מוֹרָה) תְּהֹם מְלֹא
6 שְׁלֹמֹה אַהֲרֹן יַעֲקֹב אֲדוֹן עוֹלָם
7 הַמּוֹצִיא שַׁבַּת שָׁלוֹם רֹאשׁ הַשָּׁנָה
8 תּוֹרָה בְּרָכוֹת מִצְוֹת דוֹרוֹת כֹּהֲנִים

Word Power

Circle and read the rhyming words in line 5 above.
Think about it: In Hebrew, a female teacher is called מוֹרָה. How are תּוֹרָה and מוֹרָה connected? Underline the Hebrew phrases above for:

Jewish New Year רֹאשׁ הַשָּׁנָה
a peaceful Shabbat שַׁבַּת שָׁלוֹם

CHALLENGE: Put a box around the Hebrew word meaning "no."
Hint: It is in line 1 and rhymes with no.

(54)

Figure It Out

Usually וֹ has the sound "OH" (רוֹ, צוֹן). Sometimes וֹ has the sound "VO" (צְוֹ, עֲוֹ).
Hint: If there is a vowel under the letter before וֹ, then וֹ has the sound "VO."
Read each line below. Then circle all the words in which וֹ has the sound "VO."

1 (מִצְוֹת) (עֲוֹנִי) רוֹצָה מִצְוָה רָצוֹן
2 (עֲוֹנֹתַי) (בְּמִצְוֹתַי) אַרְצוֹת (בְּמִצְוֹת) וְצִוָּנוּ
3 (עָוֹן) מַצּוֹת מִצְרָע (בְּמִצְוֹתַי) מִצְוֹת
4 (מִצְוֹתַי) (עֲוֹנָה) צָוָה מִצְיוֹן בְּרָצוֹן

Reading Rule

When the vowel וֹ is followed by the letter י at the end of a word (וֹי),
say "OY" as in boy. Now, say the Hebrew phrase for "Oh my!"
אוֹי וַאֲבוֹי — with expression!

Move It and Use It

Read aloud each of these Hebrew action words.
Divide the class into two teams, א and ב. A student from team א acts out a word. If team ב guesses the word correctly, they earn a point. A student from team ב acts out another word. Continue until all the words have been used or all students have had a turn to act out a word. The team with the most points wins. *Alternative:* Do the activity in pairs.

לְהוֹצִיא	לַעֲצוֹר	לְהוֹרִיד	לִכְתּוֹב	לִקְרוֹא
to take out	to stop	to lower	to write	to read

לְהִשְׁתַּחֲווֹת	לְהָרִים	לִמְצוֹא	לִשְׁמוֹעַ	לִרְקוֹד
to bow down	to raise	to find	to hear	to dance

(55)

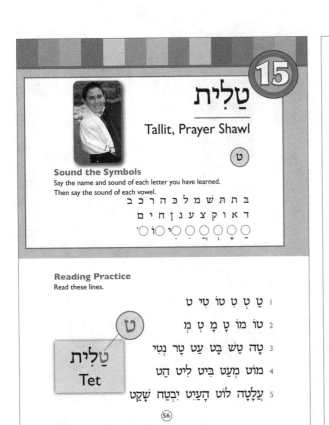

15

טַלִּית

Tallit, Prayer Shawl

ט

Sound the Symbols

Say the name and sound of each letter you have learned.
Then say the sound of each vowel.

ב ת ת ש מ ל כ ה ר כ ב
ד ט א ו ק צ ע נ ן ח י ם

◌ֹ ◌וֹ ◌ִי ◌ֵ ◌ַ ◌ָ ◌ְ ◌ֶ

Reading Practice
Read these lines.

1 טַ טְ טֹ טוֹ טְי ט

2 טוֹ מוֹ טָ מָ טְ מְ

3 טָה טַשׁ בָּט עַט טָר נְטִי

4 מוֹט מְעַט בֵּיט לִיט הַט

5 עֲלָטָה לוֹט הָעַיִט יִבְטַח שָׁקֵט

טַלִּית
Tet
ט

Reading Practice
Read the words below.

1 טוֹן טִיב מָט אַט חַיָּט מוֹטוֹ

2 טוֹב טַל אִטִי טָרִי שׁוֹט קָט

3 מִטָה מוֹט (קָטָן) חִטָה שָׁחַט לָטַשׁ

4 לְאַט מָטָר חָטָא מְעַט שֵׁבֶט בֶּטַח

5 (טַלִּית) טָהוֹר אָטָד טַעַם טִבְעִי טָמָן

6 (קְטַנָה) עֲטָרָה מִקְלָט חֲטָאִים הַבִּיטָה

7 שְׁבָטִים טוֹבִים בִּטָחוֹן נְטִילַת יָדַיִם

8 (טַלִּית) (שָׁנָה) (טוֹבָה) יוֹם טוֹב

Word Power
Can you find these Hebrew words above? Circle, then read them.

tallit, prayer shawl טַלִּית   holiday, festival יוֹם טוֹב
Happy New Year שָׁנָה טוֹבָה

CHALLENGE: In Hebrew, when a boy is small, we say he is קָטָן. And when a girl is small, we say she is קְטַנָה. In the lines above, circle these two Hebrew words for "small."

Tongue Twisters
Practice ע and צ by reading each line below.

1 צוֹ צְוֹ עוֹ עֲוֹ עוֹ צוֹ עוֹ צְוֹ

2 רָצוֹן מִצְוֹת עוֹלָם עוֹן לִנְטוֹעַ

3 צָדֵק עוֹנִי בְּמִצְוֹת לַעֲצֹם מַצוֹת

4 מִצְיוֹן בְּמִצְוֹתָיו עוֹנָה מִצְוֹתַי

5 צָמֵא צַעַד קָרַע עָתִיד

Mem-Tet Tuning
Take turns reading the words on each line. Watch out for look-alike letters, especially מ and ט!

1 מִצְרַיִם מַעֲרִיב לְמַטָה נְטִילַת הַמַמְלָכָה

2 הָעַמִּים בֶּטַח מָרוֹר מַטְבִּילִין לְמַדְתָ

3 קְטַנִים לְאַט מְצָדָה מְגִילוֹת מִטְבָּח

Reading Rule
Sometimes the vowel ◌ָ is pronounced "OH."

כָּל קָדְשׁוֹ מִכָּל עָבְדוֹ בְּכָל תָּכְנִית

16

אֱמֶת

Truth

◌ֱ ◌ֶ

Sound the Symbols

Say the name and sound of each letter you have learned.
Then say the sound of each vowel.

ב ת ת ש מ ל כ ה ר כ ב
ד א ו ק צ ע נ ן ח י ם ט

◌ֹ ◌וֹ ◌ִי ◌ֵ ◌ַ ◌ָ ◌ְ ◌ֶ

Reading Practice
Read these lines.

1 דְ בֱ טֱ אֱ יֱ

2 שְ עֱ מֶ לֱ קֱ צֶ

3 תֶם עֶד רַב חֱלִי דֱשׁ יֶה

4 צַוֶה אֶל מוֹנֶה הֶח מֶשׁ כֶּל

5 שֶל כֶּלֶב מֶרֶד שֶׁלוֹ לֶן

אֱמֶת

◌ֱ ◌ֶ

Reading Practice
Read the words below.

1. אֶת אֵל שֶׁלִי שֶׁלֹּא אֱמֶת אַתֶּן
2. אֲשֶׁר שֶׁמֶשׁ יֶלֶד לָכֶם אֹהֶל אֶבֶן
3. אַתֶּם נֶצַח חֹדֶשׁ כֹּתֶל טֶרֶם אֶחָד
4. רוֹצֶה שֶׁבַע עֶרֶב (מוֹרֶה) נֶאֱמָן יִהְיֶה
5. וְנֶאֱמַר מְחַיֶּה רוֹעֶה עוֹלֶה הֶחֱלִיט שְׁמוֹנֶה
6. לְעוֹלָם וָעֶד תּוֹרַת אֱמֶת מִצְוָה אֶתְכֶם
7. (אֲרוֹן הַקֹּדֶשׁ) כֶּתֶר תּוֹרָה וַיֹּאמֶר (אֱלֹהִים)
8. (אֱלֹהִים) (הַמּוֹצִיא לֶחֶם) אֱמֶת וְצֶדֶק

Word Power
Can you find these Hebrew words above? Circle, then read them.

teacher (masculine) מוֹרֶה   the Holy Ark אֲרוֹן הַקֹּדֶשׁ
who brings forth bread הַמּוֹצִיא לֶחֶם   God אֱלֹהִים

CHALLENGE: You might see a king or queen—or a Torah—wearing a כֶּתֶר. Read and underline the Hebrew word above. The English word for כֶּתֶר is Crown.

(60)

Word Sleuth: The Case of the Vanishing Vav
You can find the "VO" sound in ten of the words below.
1 Draw a box around the words that contain the "VO" sound.
2 Draw a triangle around the words that contain the "O" sound.
3 Circle the words that contain the "V" sound.
4 Double underline the two words that contain both a "V" and a "VO" sound.

1. צֹה (מִצְוָה) מַצּוֹת (מִצְוָה) מִצְווֹת
2. צוֹם (הַמִּצְוָה) בְּמִצְווֹת (דָּוִד) בְּמִצְוֹתַי
3. עָוֹן עוֹנָה עוֹנָה (רָצוֹן) עֲווֹנוֹת
4. וְעָוֹן לִשְׁבּוֹר הַמִּצְוֹת עֲווֹנִי בְּמִצְוֹתָי

Reading Rules:
The vowel ◌ֳ is always pronounced "OH."

אֳנִיָּה   עֳנִי   חֳדָשִׁים
עֳמָרִים   אֳרָנִים   שֳׁרָשִׁים

When the vowel ◌ comes before the vowel ◌ both vowels are pronounced "OH."

אֳהָלִים   צֳהָרַיִם   מָחֳרַת
נָעֳמִי   צֳהָלָה   מָחֳרָתַיִם

(61)

פֶּסַח (17)
Passover
(ס) (פ)

Sound the Symbols
Say the name and sound of each letter you have learned.
Then say the sound of each vowel.

ב כ ר ה כ ל מ שׁ ת ת ב
ד ו ק צ ע נ י ח מ ט

Reading Practice
Read these lines.

(פ)
פֶּסַח
Pay

1. פוֹ פֶ פַ פְּ פִּ פָ
2. פֶּה פְּרִי פֹּה פֵּן פַּת פְּתִי
3. אֵפוֹ פִּיל פָּנָה פַּחַד פֶּרַח
4. טִפָּה פָּתַח כַּפִּית פַּעַם פֶּרֶק

(62)

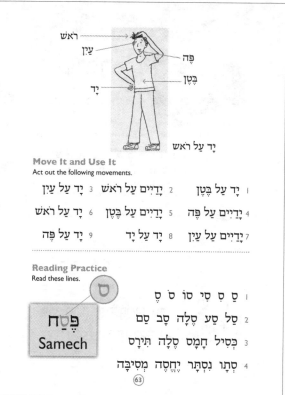

רֹאשׁ
עַיִן
פֶּה
בֶּטֶן
יָד

יָד עַל רֹאשׁ

Move It and Use It
Act out the following movements.

1 יָד עַל בֶּטֶן   2 יָדַיִם עַל רֹאשׁ   3 יָד עַל עַיִן
4 יָדַיִם עַל פֶּה   5 יָדַיִם עַל בֶּטֶן   6 יָד עַל רֹאשׁ
7 יָדַיִם עַל עַיִן   8 יָד עַל יָד   9 יָד עַל פֶּה

Reading Practice
Read these lines.

(ס)
פֶּסַח
Samech

1. סַ ס סִי סוֹ ס סְ
2. סַל סַע סֶלָה סָב סַם
3. כְּסִיל חָמָס סֶלַע תִּירֹס
4. סָתוּ נִסְתַּר יַחֲסֶה מְסִיבָּה

(63)

Reading Practice
Read the words below.

1   כּוֹס סֶלַע מַס פֶּסַח סְתָו סִיָן

2   סְתָם חֶסֶד סַבָּא סַבְתָּא חָסִיד כַּסְפּוֹ

3   נִיסָן סְדְרָה חַסְדוֹ סַנְדָק יְסוֹד מִסְפָּר

4   מַסֹרֶת נִסִים נִכְנָס כְּסוֹד מְנַסֶּה לַעֲסֹק

5   סְבִיבוֹן מִסָבִיב בָּסִיס הִסְפִּיד וְנִסְכּוֹ מַחְסִי

6   מְסַפֶּרֶת כְּנֶסֶת נִסְפָּה הַכְנָסַת מַסְפִּיק

7   חֲסִידִים חֲסִידִים פַּרְנָסָה סְלִיחָה סְלִיחוֹת

8   פֶּסַח (כַּרְפַּס) (חֲרוֹסֶת) (מַצָּה) (מָרוֹר) פֶּסַח

Word Power
In the lines above, read and circle the Hebrew words for foods we eat on Passover:
מַצָּה כַּרְפַּס מָרוֹר חֲרוֹסֶת
Underline פֶּסַח, the Hebrew name for Passover.

CHALLENGE: On which line is the Hebrew word for dreidel? __5__

(64)

Sound Off
Take turns reading the words on each line. Watch out for look-alike letters, especially ס and ם!

1   פְּעָמִים עֲרָבִים חֲסָדִים בְּשָׁמַיִם נִסִים

2   רַחֲמִים מַסְבִּיר סֹב סוֹבְבִים רָסִיס

3   סַפִּיר הָרִים סַהַר הַשָּׁמַיִם יַחְסֹר

4   סוֹדוֹת יִרְעַם כִּסְאוֹ לָהֶם רְשָׁעִים

Eating in Israel
Imagine you're in a supermarket in Israel. Now read aloud the names of different foods. Circle the ones you recognize. Fun Fact: If you ask for סוֹדָה in Israel, you'll get seltzer!

1   בָּנָנָה פּוֹפְּקוֹרְן קוֹלָה פִּיצָה פִּיתָה

2   סַיְדֶר שׁוֹקוֹלָד אָבוֹקָדוֹ סוֹדָה בְּרוֹקוֹלִי

3   קִיוִי נֶקְטָרִינָה אַרְטִישׁוֹק לִימוֹן פַּפְרִיקָה

Letter Marathon
Take turns reading the words on each line. Watch out for more look-alike letters, especially ט and מ, and ס and ם!

1   מְצָדָה חַטָּה מְסִירָה מַחֲנֶה רוֹמָאִי

2   מִלְחָמָה מֶלַח טוֹבִים סֶלָה רְהִיטִים

3   כִּמְעַט עָסִיס יָטֹשׁ עֲטָרָה מַסָּה

(65)

18

שׁוֹפָר

Shofar

פ

Sound the Symbols
Say the name and sound of each letter you have learned. Then say the sound of each vowel.

ב ת ת ש מ ל כ ה ר כ ב ד
א ו ק צ ע נ ן ח י ם ס
◯ ◌ ◌ ◌ ◌ ◌ ◌ ◌ ◌

Reading Practice
Read these lines.

פ

1   פִּי פֶּ פַּ פּוֹ פִּ פֹּ

2   פֶּ פֵּ פְּ פָּ פֹּ פֹּ

שׁוֹפָר
Fay

3   יוֹפִי נַפְשִׁי יָפָה פַּרְעֹה נִפְלָא

4   לְפָנָיו הָפַכְתָּ עֲפָרִים פָּעֳלִי פֶּסֶל

(66)

Reading Practice
Read the words below.

1   יָפֶה עָפָר כַּפִּי נֶפֶשׁ חֹפֶשׁ צוֹפֶה

2   אַפִּי תָפַס נָפַל אָפָה יָמִים נַפְשִׁי

3   אֹפֶן אֶפֶס צָפוֹן שֶׁפַע כֹּפֶר יִפְתֶּה

4   אָסַפְתָּ אֶפְשָׁר (תְּפִלָּה) מַפְטִיר תִּפְתַּח לִפְעָמִים

5   תְּפִלּוֹת (סְפָרִים) סוֹפְרִים לִפְנִים צוֹפִיָה אַפְקִיד

6   לִפְדוֹת נוֹפְלִים טוֹטָפֹת נַפְשְׁכֶם תִּפְאֶרֶת

7   אֲפִיקוֹמָן (הַפְטָרָה) שׁוֹפְטִים כְּמִפְעָלוֹ תְּפִלִין

8   שׁוֹפָר (תְּפִלָּה) תְּפִלִין מַפְטִיר (הַפְטָרָה)

Word Power
Can you find these Hebrew words above? Circle, then read them.
prayer תְּפִלָּה   Haftarah הַפְטָרָה   books סְפָרִים

CHALLENGE: Read and underline the Hebrew word for the half piece of matzah we search for—and find—during the פֶּסַח seder.

(67)

Partner Help

Read these lines. Circle any words you are having trouble with. Ask a study partner to help you. Give yourself a smiley face for each circled word you read correctly.

1. פִּיּוֹת   פֶּרַח   פְּרִי   פְּרָחִים
2. כַּפָּה   אַפַּיִם   פְּנֵי   מַפָּה
3. עֶפְרוֹן   פֹּה   פֶּן   רִצְפָּה
4. לְטֹטָפֹת   תְּפִלּוֹת   אֶפְשָׁר   אוֹפֶה
5. דָּפַק   תְּפִלִּין   מוֹפְתִים   בְּפִי
6. וְאָסַפְתָּ   הַקָּפָּה   פֶּלֶא   פָּדָה

Tzadee-Ayin Warm-Up

Take turns reading the five lines.

1. עֲצֵי צוֹצֵ עֵצָ צוֹעוֹ
2. צַעֲי עֵצָ צוֹצוֹ עֲצֵי
3. צָן עֲי צְו עֵינִי
4. צִיאָ צְנוּ צִיוֹ צוֹף
5. עֵצוֹ עֵן עַם עֵטֵע

₆₈

עֵץ חַיִּים
Tree of Life

Sound the Symbols

Say the name and sound of each letter you have learned.
Then say the sound of each vowel.

א ב כ ד ב כ ר ה כ מ ל ש ת ת ב
פ ס פ ט מ י ח נ ע צ ק ו

Reading Practice

Read these lines.

1. שֶׁ פֵּי מֵי לִי דַ נִי
2. פֵּי סֶ טֵי יֵי עִי כֵּ
3. כֹּה אוֹמֵ הֵיט דְּרֵי
4. סֵפֶר כֹּהֵן אוֹמֵר הֵיטִיב
5. בְּנֵי שְׁנֵי בְּצֵאת חַיֵּיהֶם

עֵץ חַיִּים

₆₉

Rhyme Time

Read each line below aloud.
Circle, then read, the two rhyming words aloud.

1. בֵּן נֵר תֵּל כֵּן
2. אָמַר אָמֵן שֶׁמֶן עָמַר
3. קוֹרֵא תּוֹקֵעַ שׁוֹמֵר שׁוֹמֵעַ
4. מִנְיָן מִקְוָה בִּנְיָן בָּנִים
5. טָהֵר טוֹבָה מַהֵר מִצְוָה

Reading Practice

Read these lines.

Final Tzadee

1. עֵץ קֵץ חֵץ רָץ אָץ נֵץ
2. עֵץ עֵצִים רָץ רָצָה לֵץ לֵיצָן
3. חֵן קֵן אֲצֵי דִין אֵין קַיִץ

Move It and Use It

Describe a time when someone told you: לֹא לִקְפּוֹץ or לִקְפּוֹץ
Which did you want to do? לֹא לִקְפּוֹץ or לִקְפּוֹץ

₇₀

Reading Practice

Read the words below.

1. אֶרֶץ חָמֵץ מַצָּה חָפֵץ קַיִץ
2. קוֹץ קוֹצִים בּוֹץ פֶּרֶץ קוֹפֵץ
3. נוֹצֵץ לוֹחֵץ צִנְחָן עֵצִי מִיץ
4. אֹמֶץ אֶמְצַע מֶרֶץ אַמִּיץ הֵצִיץ
5. אֱלֹהֵי פִּרְקֵי נִדְרֵי אַחֲרֵי חַסְדֵי תִּשְׁרֵי
6. עֵץ חַיִּים הַמּוֹצִיא לֶחֶם מִן הָאָרֶץ

Word Power

On Passover, we eat מַצָּה but not חָמֵץ, "leavened food." Find and circle those two words above.

We call the Torah עֵץ חַיִּים, a "Tree of Life." In the lines above, find this phrase and draw a Torah around the Hebrew words.

CHALLENGE: Put a rectangle around the phrase in line 6 that is the ending of the blessing recited before eating חַלָּה.

₇₁

That's Final

Five Hebrew letters change their form when they appear at the end of a word. You have learned three so far.

מ ם	ץ צ	ן נ

Read aloud the following prayer phrases. Circle each word that ends with a letter that has a changed final form. Now read aloud each of the circled words.

1 אֵת הַשָּׁמַיִם וְאֵת הָאָרֶץ

2 כִּי מִצִּיוֹן תֵּצֵא תוֹרָה

3 וַיָּרֶם קֶרֶן לְעַמּוֹ

4 קוֹנֵה שָׁמַיִם וָאָרֶץ

5 בַּשָּׁמַיִם מִמַּעַל וְעַל הָאָרֶץ מִתָּחַת

6 אֲשֶׁר הוֹצֵאתִי אֶתְכֶם מֵאֶרֶץ מִצְרָיִם

Move It and Use It

Read each of the Hebrew words aloud. Now circle the names of items you see in your classroom. Stand up and touch each item as you say its name.

רִצְפָּה	חַלּוֹן	דֶּלֶת	קִיר	כִּסֵּא	סֵפֶר
floor	window	door	wall	chair	book

עִפָּרוֹן	מַחְשֵׁב	מַחְבֶּרֶת	עֵט	מִסְפָּרַיִם	מַחַק
eraser	computer	notebook	pen	scissors	pencil

(72)

20

יִשְׂרָאֵל

Israel

Sound the Symbols

ש

Say the name and sound of each letter you have learned. Then say the sound of each vowel.

ב ת ת ש ש מ ל כ ה ר כ ב ד א

ו ק צ ע נ ח י ם ט פ ס פ ץ

◌ָ ◌ֶ ◌ַ ◌ֵ ◌ִ יִ וֹ וּ ◌ֻ ◌ַ ◌ֻ ◌ַ י

Reading Practice

Read these lines.

1 שָׁ שִׁי שִׁ שׁוֹ שָׁ שֶׁ

2 שֶׁ שֵׁ שִׁי שׁוֹ שִׁי שׁוּ

3 נִשְׂמַח עֶשֶׂב שָׂמְתֶּם פּוֹרֵשׂ

4 שְׂפָתַי וְיִתְנַשֵּׂא יַעֲשֶׂה יִשְׂמַח

ש

יִשְׂרָאֵל
Sin

(73)

Reading Practice

Read the words below.

1 שֶׂה שִׂים שַׂר שָׂם שַׂק שִׂיא

2 שָׂרָה שָׂנֵא שָׂמַח עֶשֶׂר עֹשֶׂה מַשָּׂא

3 שָׂרָה שָׂרָה שָׂמָה שָׂמָה שֵׂעָר שָׂשׂוֹן

4 שֵׂעָר שָׂכָר שָׂפָה יִשָּׂא בָּשָׂר שֵׂכֶל

5 שָׂדֶה פָּשַׁט עֶשֶׂר שֶׁבַע עָשָׂה תַּיִשׁ

6 שִׂמְחַת תּוֹרָה שְׁמוֹנָה עֲשָׂרָה עֲשֶׂרֶת הַדִּבְּרוֹת

7 שְׁמַע יִשְׂרָאֵל שִׂים שָׁלוֹם עוֹשֶׂה שָׁלוֹם

8 עַם יִשְׂרָאֵל בְּנֵי יִשְׂרָאֵל אֶרֶץ יִשְׂרָאֵל

Word Power

Find and circle the Hebrew for these numbers above:

שְׁמוֹנָה עֲשָׂרָה 18	עֶשֶׂר 10	שֶׁבַע 7

CHALLENGE: Underline אֶרֶץ יִשְׂרָאֵל (the Land of Israel).
Name a city in אֶרֶץ יִשְׂרָאֵל.

(74)

Shin-Sin Warm-Up

Pay attention to שׁ (sh) and שׂ (s) as you read each line.

1 שַׁ שָׂ שֵׁ שֵׂ שׁ

2 שֶׁ שֵׂ שִׁי שַׂ שׂ

3 שֵׁשׁ שָׂשׂ שַׂב שָׂר רַשׁ

4 לָשִׂים שׁוֹמֵעַ קֹדֶשׁ רֹאשׁ שִׂמְחָה

5 לַעֲשׂוֹת שֶׁעָשָׂה לָשֶׁבֶת עָשָׂה אֲחַשְׁוֵרוֹשׁ

Reading Rule

Some dots do double duty. They indicate the vowel sound "O" *and* whether the letter שׁ makes a "S" or a "SH" sound. Practice reading these words.

שֹׁנְאַי נְחֹשֶׁת נָשָׂא שֹׁשָׁן שָׁלֹשׁ מֹשֶׁה

Move It and Use It

Stand up and read each Hebrew word below. As you read, walk around the room according to the Hebrew direction. When, for example, you read קָדִימָה, step forward. Have fun taking turns and directing where your friends should walk.

go forward קָדִימָה	go to the left שְׂמֹאלָה
here פֹּה	go to the right יְמִינָה
go back אֲחוֹרָה	

(75)

21

חַג שָׂמֵחַ

Happy Holiday

ג

Sound the Symbols
Say the name and sound of each letter you have learned.
Then say the sound of each vowel.

ב ת ת ש מ ל כ כ ה ר כ ב ד א
ו ק צ ע נ ן ח י ה ם ט פ ס פ ץ ש

◯ ◯ ◯ ◯ ◯ ◯ י◯ ◯ו◯ ◯ ◯ ◯ ◯ ◯ ◯ ◯ י◯

Reading Practice
Read these lines.

ג

חַג שָׂמֵחַ
Gimmel

1 גַ גוֹ גֶ גַ גֶ גִי

2 גַג גָלוֹ גַבֵּי גַנֵי גִיס גִיר

3 גֹּלֶם מָגֵן גִּבּוֹר עֹנֶג גֶּשֶׁם

4 אֶתְרוֹג נָגִילָה שִׁגָּעוֹן יִתְגַּדַל

(76)

Reading Rule
When חַ is at the end of a word, say "ACH" as in "ko-ach" (כֹּחַ).
Read these lines.

1 כֹּחַ מֹחַ רֵיחַ נֹחַ שִׂיחַ בְּכַחַ

2 יָרֵחַ בַּכֹּחַ לְנֹחַ כְּשִׂיחַ לִשְׁכֹּחַ

3 מוֹחַ נִיחוֹחַ נוֹחַ לְהָנִיחַ מִשְׁתַּבֵּחַ

Prayer Building Blocks
Read these siddur phrases.
Put a check next to each phrase that you read correctly.

_____ עָלֵינוּ לְשַׁבֵּחַ לַאֲדוֹן הַכֹּל

_____ הָאֵל הַגָּדוֹל הַגִּבּוֹר וְהַנּוֹרָא

_____ לְעֵת תָּכִין מַטְבֵּחַ

_____ לְהוֹדוֹת לְהַלֵּל לְשַׁבֵּחַ

_____ שְׂמֵחִים בְּצֵאתָם וְשָׂשִׂים בְּבוֹאָם

Read these endings to familiar בְּרָכוֹת (blessings). When do we recite each one?

1 בּוֹרֵא פְּרִי הַגָּפֶן *over wine or grape juice*
4 בּוֹרֵא פְּרִי הָעֵץ *over fruit*

2 בּוֹרֵא פְּרִי הָאֲדָמָה *over vegetables*
5 בּוֹרֵא מְאוֹרֵי הָאֵשׁ *over Havdalah candle*

3 בּוֹרֵא מִינֵי בְשָׂמִים *over spices*
6 הַמּוֹצִיא לֶחֶם מִן הָאָרֶץ *over bread*

(77)

Reading Practice
Read the words below.

1 חַן גַן גְּדִי גֵּר דָּג גַם

2 גִּבּוֹר גּוֹלֵל גּוֹמֵל גָּאַל גֶּשֶׁם דֶּגֶל

3 שָׂמֵחַ יָרֵחַ אוֹרֵחַ נָשִׁיחַ מֵנִיחַ בַּכֹּחַ

4 לְשַׁבֵּחַ מְנַצֵּחַ שׁוֹלֵחַ מָנוֹחַ שָׁלִיחַ מַפְתֵּחַ

5 גּוֹלָה מְגִילָה הִשִּׂיג מִנְהָג גָּדוֹל גְּטִים

6 מָשִׁיחַ חַג שָׂמֵחַ פֶּסַח הַגָּדָה מְגִילָה

7 אַגָּדָה אֶתְרוֹג רֶגֶל הִגְדִּיל חַגִּים גְּדוֹלָה

8 הַגָּדָה חַד גַּדְיָא מָגֵן דָּוִד מָגֵן אָבוֹת

Word Power
Put a circle around the Hebrew word above for the book we read from at the פֶּסַח seder.
Draw a קַו (line) under the Hebrew word for the text we read on Purim.

CHALLENGE: Put a box around חַג שָׂמֵחַ, the Hebrew greeting for a happy holiday. Name two occasions when we say this greeting.

(78)

Move It and Use It
big גְּדוֹלָה, גָּדוֹל small קָטָן, קְטַנָּה

Read these phrases. Then draw a line from each phrase to its matching picture.

שׁוֹפָר גָּדוֹל   שׁוֹפָר קָטָן   תּוֹרָה קְטַנָּה   תּוֹרָה גְּדוֹלָה   שׁוֹפָר קָטָן

Rhyme Time
Connect the rhyming words.

נוֹדֶה — ללֶכֶת
גּוֹמֵל — עַמִּים
לוֶוה — עַתָּה
בֵּין — לָרֶדֶת
שָׁתָה — אוֹכֵל
תָּמִים — אֵין

Samech-Sin Warm-Up
Pay attention to שׂ and ס as you read each line.

1 חֶסֶד כּוֹסִי שְׂמֵחִים פַּרְנָסָה שָׂשׂוֹן

2 אֶסְתֵּר מִתְנַשְּׂאִים יְסֹב נִסִּי פֶּסַח

(79)

22 קִדּוּשׁ

Kiddush

וּ

Sound the Symbols

Say the name and sound of each letter you have learned.
Then say the sound of each vowel.

ב ת ת שׁ שׂ מ ל כ כ ה ר כ ב ד א ו
ק צ ע נ ן ח י ה מ ט פ ף ס פּ שׁ י ג

◯ ◯ ◯ ◯ ◯ ◯ ◯ י◯ י◯וּ◯ ◯י ◯ ◯ ◯ ◯ ◯ ◯
◯ֵ◌י

Reading Practice

Read these lines.

וּ

1 סוּ שׁוּ טוּ נוּ מוּ צוּ

2 בְּ גְ שְׁ רְ קְ תְּ

3 הוּא לָנוּ אָנוּ בָּנוּ צוּד כֻּלוֹ

4 שׁוּם סֻכַּת וּבְכָל לָקוּם כֻּלָּם

קִדּוּשׁ
Kiddush
◯ ◌וּ

(80)

Reading Practice

Read the words below.

1 חָמֵשׁ (לוּחַ) כֻּלָּם וְהָיוּ סֻכָּה טֹבוּ

2 עָלֵינוּ לְבֵנוּ סֻכּוֹת שָׁבוּעַ חֲנֻכָּה קָבוּץ

3 קָדוֹשׁ (שֻׁלְחָן) מִשְׁבָּח סָדוּר מִצְיָן כֻּלָּנוּ

4 הַלְלוּיָהּ גְּדֻלָּה פָּסוּק יְשׁוּעָה נְטוּיָה אֲנַחְנוּ

5 וּבְנַחֲה לוֹלָב וְיָפְצוּ וַיִּכְלוּ וְיָנֻסוּ דַּיֵּנוּ

6 תְּמוּנָה וְרָצֵנוּ אֵלֶיהוּ הַנָּבִיא בָּרְכוּ קְשִׁיּוֹת

7 קָדְשָׁה יְהוּדִים פּוּרִים יוֹם כִּפּוּר שָׁבוּעוֹת

8 יְרוּשָׁלַיִם אֱלֹהֵינוּ שֶׁהֶחֱיָנוּ אָבִינוּ מַלְכֵּנוּ

Word Power

Some Hebrew words have more than one meaning.
שֻׁלְחָן is a desk or a table.
A לוּחַ can be a chalkboard, bulletin board, or even a calendar.
Read and circle לוּחַ and שֻׁלְחָן in the lines above.

(81)

Oh-Oo Warm-Up

Be alert for the vowels וֹ and וּ as you read each line aloud.
Time yourself, then try to beat your own best time.

1 יוֹם טוֹב תּוֹרָה שָׁלוֹם בּוֹרֵא עוֹלָם

2 הוּא צוּר לָנוּ בָּנוּ דַּיֵּינוּ אֲנַחְנוּ פּוּרִים

3 גָּדוֹל גּוֹאֵל צִיּוֹן סִדּוּר קִדּוּשׁ קָדוֹשׁ

4 וּבְכָל וּמַה הוֹדוּ מַלְכוּתוֹ אֲדוֹנֵינוּ

Reading Rule

When the vowel וּ is followed by the letter י at the end of a word, say
"OOEY" as in gooey.

צִוּוּי קָנוּי עָשׂוּי רָצוּי גָּלוּי וְדוּי פָּנוּי בָּנוּי

Word Play

Form a group of three. The first person reads the first word part (קוּף).
The second person reads the second word part (סָה). The third person
reads the whole word (קוּפְסָה). Continue in that way.

1 קוּף סָה קוּפְסָה	6 לַס גּוּר לַסְגּוּר	
2 לַ רוּץ לָרוּץ	7 וּמַב דִּיל וּמַבְדִּיל	
3 וַאֲנַח נוּ וַאֲנַחְנוּ	8 בֵּי צָה בֵּיצָה	
4 גֻּ שֶׁם גֻּשֶׁם	9 קָ דוּשׁ קָדוּשׁ	
5 יִת גַּדֵּל יִתְגַּדֵּל	10 כְּגוֹ יֵי כְּגוֹיֵי	

(82)

Sing Along

Read and then sing this popular holiday song.
On which holiday do we sing it? _Hanukkah_

סְבִיבוֹן סֹב סֹב סֹב. חֲנֻכָּה הוּא חַג טוֹב.
חֲנֻכָּה הוּא חַג טוֹב. סְבִיבוֹן סֹב סֹב סֹב.

Power Reading

Practice reading these phrases from the קִדּוּשׁ. Put a check next to all
the phrases that you read correctly.

1 אֲשֶׁר קִדְּשָׁנוּ בְּמִצְוֹתָיו וְרָצָה בָנוּ

2 כִּי הוּא יוֹם תְּחִלָּה לְמִקְרָאֵי קֹדֶשׁ

3 כִּי בָנוּ בָחַרְתָּ וְאוֹתָנוּ קִדַּשְׁתָּ

4 בְּאַהֲבָה וּבְרָצוֹן הִנְחַלְתָּנוּ

5 מְקַדֵּשׁ הַשַּׁבָּת

Double Sh'va (◌ְ) Toss

When ◌ְ appears under two consecutive letters, the first ◌ְ has no
sound. It tells you to STOP. The second ◌ְ makes a short "UH" sound.
It lets you GO. Practice reading these words with double sh'vas. Draw a
line to indicate the STOP.

1 מִשְׁפְּטֵי אַרְבְּכָה בְּמִשְׁפְּחוֹת יִשְׁמְעוּ

2 יִשְׂמְחוּ יְלַמְּדוּ תִּשְׁמְרוּ יְסַפְּרוּ בְּמִשְׁמְרוֹתֵיהֶם

(83)

23

מְזוּזָה
Mezuzah

ז

Sound the Symbols

Say the name and sound of each letter you have learned.
Then say the sound of each vowel.

ב ת ת ש מ ל כ ה ר כ ב ד א ו

ק צ ע נ ן ח י ם ט פ ס פ ץ ש ׳ ג

◯ ◯ ◯ ◯ ◯ ◯וֹ ◯ ◯ ◯וֹ ◯ ◯ ◯ ◯וּ ◯ ◯ ◯ ◯

Reading Practice

Read these lines. Be alert! The first ◯ in both of the words on line 4 has the sound "OH."

ז

מְזוּזָה
Zayin

1 זָ זוּ זוֹ זִ זֵ זֶ

2 זֶ שֶ ַ ס זִ צ

3 זוֹכֵר עוֹזֵר וּבִזְמַן תִּזְכְּרוּ

4 זָכְרֵנוּ אָזְנֵי־הָמָן

(84)

Reading Practice

Read the words below.

1 זֶה אָז עֹז פָּז בּוּז זָר

2 זָכֹר זְמַן אֹזֶן חָזָק חַזָן אָחַז

3 הַזָן זֶבַח זֹאת מַזָל זָקֵן זָהָב

4 יִזְכֹּר מָעוֹז זֵכֶר אֵיזֶה עֻזֵנוּ וְזַרְעוֹ

5 זִכָּרוֹן מִזְבֵּחַ (מַחֲזוֹר) מִזְמוֹר נֶעֱזָב זַיִת

6 זְכוּת מִזְרָח זְרוֹעַ מָזוֹן זַרְעָם עִזִים

7 זַיִת הֶחֱזִיר זָקוּק הִזְנִיחַ חָזָק וְאֱמָץ

8 (מְזוּזָה) יוֹם הַזִכָּרוֹן (מַחֲזוֹר) (מַזָל טוֹב)

Word Power

Can you find these Hebrew words above? Circle, then read them.

congratulations מַזָל טוֹב   mezuzah מְזוּזָה
machzor מַחֲזוֹר

CHALLENGE: Name an occasion when we say מַזָל טוֹב.

_____

(85)

Repairing the World

When we care for the environment and all living things, we are engaged in תִּקוּן עוֹלָם. How do you do תִּקוּן עוֹלָם?

Vav-Zayin Relay Race

Take turns reading the words. Watch out for look-alike letters!

1 אַזַי וְצַוֵנוּ וְזֹאת מָזוֹן

2 וְזִמְרָת מְזוּזָה חָזָק קוֹינוּ

3 וְעָזוּז זִכָּרוֹן מְזוֹנוֹת גּוִיָתִי

4 בַּזְמַן זִכְרוֹנֵנוּ כַּוָנָה אֲרָזִים

5 הַזָן רַעֲוָא זֵכֶר וּמִשְׁתַּחֲוִים

Great Greetings

Match the Hebrew greeting to its proper occasion.

שָׁבוּעַ טוֹב! שַׁבַּת שָׁלוֹם! חַג שָׂמֵחַ! מַזָל טוֹב!

(86)

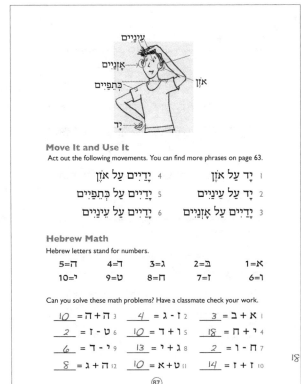

עֵינַיִם
אָזְנַיִם
כְּתֵפַיִם
אֹזֶן
יָד

Move It and Use It

Act out the following movements. You can find more phrases on page 63.

1 יָד עַל אֹזֶן   4 יָדַיִם עַל אֹזֶן

2 יָד עַל עֵינַיִם   5 יָדַיִם עַל כְּתֵפַיִם

3 יָדַיִם עַל אָזְנַיִם   6 יָדַיִם עַל עֵינַיִם

Hebrew Math

Hebrew letters stand for numbers.

1=א	2=ב	3=ג	4=ד	5=ה
6=ו	7=ז	8=ח	9=ט	10=י

Can you solve these math problems? Have a classmate check your work.

1 א + ב = _3_   2 יב - ג = _4_   3 ה + ה = _10_

4 י + ח = _18_   5 ו + ד = _10_   6 ט - ז = _2_

7 ח - ו = _2_   8 י + ג = _13_   9 י - ד = _6_

10 ז + ז = _14_   11 ט+א = _10_   12 ה + ג = _8_

18

(87)

24

בָּרוּךְ

Praised, Blessed

ךְ

Sound the Symbols
Say the name and sound of each letter you have learned.
Then say the sound of each vowel.

ב ת ת ש מ ל מ כ ה ר כ ב ד א ו
ק צ ע נ ן ח י ם ט פ ס פ ץ שׁ ג ז

◯וּ◯וֹ◯ ◯ ◯ ◯ ◯ ◯י ◯י ◯ ◯ ◯ ◯

Reading Practice
Read these lines.

1 רַךְ כַּךְ בָּךְ לֵךְ לְךָ יֵלֵךְ
2 אַךְ בְּךָ שֶׁלְךָ בְּכָה שִׁמְךָ תֵּיךְ
3 לָךְ חֹשֶׁךְ אֹרֶךְ הָלַךְ בְּרִיךְ
4 דְּגָנֶךָ בְּשָׂדְךָ שְׁמֶךָ טוֹבֶךְ אֵלֶיךָ
5 תּוֹרָתְךָ פָּנֶיךָ מָלַךְ חַסְדְּךָ בָּרוּךְ

בָּרוּךְ
Final Chaf

(88)

Reading Rule
When ךָ comes at the end of a word, the letter י is silent.
Read the words below.

חֲסָדֶיךָ   עֲבָדֶיךָ   מַעֲשֶׂיךָ   אֱלֹהֶיךָ   לְפָנֶיךָ

Reading Practice
Read the words below.

1 (בָּרוּךְ) אִמְךָ שְׁמֶךָ עַמְךָ דֶּרֶךְ עָלֶיךָ
2 (מֶלֶךְ) לִבֶּךָ רֵעֶךָ פֶּרֶךְ אֶרֶךְ לֵבָב
3 כָּמוֹךָ צָרִיךְ הוֹלֵךְ אֵלֶיךָ אָבִיךָ עֻזֶּךָ
4 (בָּרוּךְ) בָּנֶיךָ עִמְּךָ בֵּיתֶךָ אוֹתְךָ כֻּלְּךָ
5 מִבְרָךְ יִמְלֹךְ לְבָבְךָ יָדֶיךָ מְאֹדֶךָ
6 לְפָנֶיךָ עֵינֶיךָ נַפְשְׁךָ מִצְוֹתְךָ סוֹמֵךְ מַלְאָךְ
7 מִצְוֹתֶיךָ קֻדְשָׁתְךָ בִּשְׁלוֹמֶךָ אֱלֹהַיִךְ
8 תַּנֵּךְ (בָּרוּךְ) וּבְלֶכְתְּךָ וּבְקוּמֶךָ וּבִשְׁעָרֶיךָ

Word Power
Find and circle these Hebrew words above.

blessed, praised בָּרוּךְ   king, ruler מֶלֶךְ

(89)

Rhyme Time
Read aloud the Hebrew words on each line. Circle the two rhyming
words. Now read the rhyming words aloud.

1 יָדֶךְ (דֶּגֶל) בָּרוּךְ (רֶגֶל)
2 מְבֹרָךְ (תְּשׁוּבָה) (תְּרוּעָה) אָרוֹךְ
3 (סֻפְגָּנִיָּה) (חֲנֻכִּיָּה) עָלֶיךָ שְׁלוֹמֶךָ
4 שֶׁלְךָ (מִצְוָה) מֶלֶךְ (לְבָבְךָ)
5 (תְּמוּנָה) רַחֲמָיו לִכְבוֹד (עֲגֻלָּה)

Who Knows One?
These lines are from a Passover counting song. Form a pair. Read the line
with the number your partner calls out.

6 שִׁשָּׁה סִדְרֵי מִשְׁנָה   1 אֶחָד אֱלֹהֵינוּ שֶׁבַּשָּׁמַיִם וּבָאָרֶץ
7 שִׁבְעָה יְמֵי שַׁבָּתָּא   2 שְׁנֵי לוּחוֹת הַבְּרִית
8 שְׁמוֹנָה יְמֵי מִילָה   3 שְׁלֹשָׁה אָבוֹת
9 תִּשְׁעָה יַרְחֵי לֵידָה   4 אַרְבַּע אִמָּהוֹת
10 עֲשָׂרָה דִבְּרַיָּא   5 חֲמִשָּׁה חֻמְשֵׁי תוֹרָה

(90)

25

אָלֶף

Alef

פ

Sound the Symbols
Say the name and sound of each letter you have learned.
Then say the sound of each vowel.

ב ת ת ש מ ל מ כ ה ר כ ב ד א ו
ק צ ע נ ן ח י ם ט פ ס פ ץ שׁ ג ז ך

◯וּ◯וֹ◯ ◯ ◯ ◯ ◯ ◯י ◯י ◯ ◯ ◯ ◯ ◯
◯ָ

Reading Practice
Read these lines.

1 אַף דַּף עוֹף קוֹף גוּף סוּף
2 כַּף תּוֹף עָף סוֹף תַּף כֵּף
3 יֵף נָף טֵף סָף רַף צוּף
4 טָרַף אָלֶף יָעוֹף בְּתוֹף רָדַף

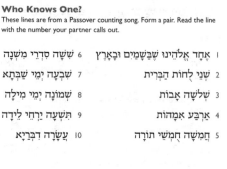

אָלֶף
Final Fay

(91)

Reading Practice
Read the words below.

1 נוֹף הַדַף חַף עָיֵף סַף חוֹף
2 חֹרֶף תֵּיכֶף עֹרֶף עָנָף כֶּסֶף שָׂרַף
3 שֶׁטֶף יוֹסֵף אָלֶף חָלַף חָלָב כָּתֵף כַּף
4 מוּסָף צָפוּף קֶלַף זוֹקֵף קוֹטֵף לָעוּף
5 אָסַף נִשְׂרַף שָׁטוּף רָצוּף כָּנָף יָחֵף
6 עַפְעַף מְרַחֵף רוֹדֵף ‏‏[שָׁלוֹם] זוֹקֵף כְּפוּפִים
7 מִצַּפְצֵף לְהִתְאַסֵף לֶאֱסֹף הֶחֱלִיף לְשַׁפְשֵׁף
8 אָלֶף בֵּית וְצִוָּנוּ (לְהִתְעַטֵף בַּצִּיצִית)

Word Power
Circle and then read the last two words of line 8 above.
Do you know which blessing has these words?

CHALLENGE: Find the Hebrew name for Joseph in the lines above.
Write the line number. __3__
Can you find the Hebrew word for *peace*? Put a box around the word.

(92)

Plant Your Roots
Most Hebrew words are built on three root letters—called the שֹׁרֶשׁ.
The word בָּרוּךְ is built on the root ברכ, which means "bless" or "praise." Write ברכ below the tree, from right to left. Circle the three root letters in each Hebrew word on the tree.

REMEMBER!
The letters ב and בּ are members of the same letter family.
The letters ך, כ, כּ are members of the same letter family.

בֵּרְכוּ בְּרָכָה
בָּרֵךְ מִבָּרֵךְ
בָּרְכוֹת יִתְבָּרַךְ
בֵּרְכוּנִי בִּרְכַּת

ב ר כ

CHALLENGE: Underline the Hebrew word for *blessing* in the tree.

Eye-Ahv March
Watch out for the endings as you read these words!

1 שַׁדַּי עָלַי אֲדֹנָי אֱלֹהַי סִינַי
2 דְּבָרַי אֲבוֹתַי וּשְׂפָתַי רַבּוֹתַי מִצְוֹתַי
3 עָלָיו עֵינָיו יָדָיו חֲסִידָיו דְּבָרָיו
4 פָּנָיו מִצְוֹתָיו בְּרַחֲמָיו מַעֲשָׂיו

(93)

Double Sh'va (ְ) Relay
Form a group of three. One person reads the first word part (נַפְ).
The second person reads the second word part (שְׁךָ).
The third person reads the whole word (נַפְשְׁךָ).
Continue that pattern.
Be alert! The first ְ in words 5 and 10 has the "OH" sound.

1 נַפְ שְׁךָ נַפְשְׁךָ 6 תִּן כְּרוּ תִּזְכְּרוּ
2 חַס דְּךָ חַסְדְּךָ 7 נַפְ שְׁכֶם נַפְשְׁכֶם
3 בְּשִׁבְ תְּךָ בְּשִׁבְתְּךָ 8 וּבְלֶכְ תְּךָ וּבְלֶכְתְּךָ
4 תִּבְ טְחוּ תִּבְטְחוּ 9 בְּצֵל צְלִי בְּצַלְצְלֵי
5 קַדְ שְׁךָ קָדְשְׁךָ 10 וּבְשָׁכְ בְּךָ וּבְשָׁכְבְּךָ

Final Letter Wrap-Up
Choose three words on each line that you'd like to practice. Next time practice the remaining three words on each line.

1 בִּכּוּרִים לָאָדוֹן תְּפִילִין סוֹף אֶרֶץ
2 אֲפִיקוֹמָן יוֹסֵף חֹשֶׁן לֶחֶם עֵץ
3 רִאשׁוֹן עוֹלָם יַם-סוּף גְּדוֹלִים בִּשְׁלוֹמֶךָ
4 פָּמוֹטִים תָּרֹדוּף לְבָרֵךְ חָלוּץ נֶאֱמָן

(94)

אָלֶף בֵּית				
ד	ג	ב	בּ	א
ט	ח	ז	ו	ה
ל	ך	כ	כּ	י
ס	ן	נ	מ	מ
צ	ף	פ	פּ	ע
שׁ	שׂ	ר	ק	ץ
			ת	תּ

(95)

Hebrew Vowels

Pronunciation	Transliteration	Name	Symbol
"ah" as in father	kamatz	קָמָץ	◌ָ
"ah" as in father	patach	פַּתָח	◌ַ
"uh" or silent	sh'va	שְׁוָא	◌ְ
"ah" as in father	chataf-patach	חֲטַף-פַּתָח	◌ֲ
"ee" as in bee	chirik	חִירִיק	◌ִ
"o" as in open	cholam	חוֹלָם	וֹ
"o" as in open	cholam chaseir	חוֹלָם-חָסֵר	◌ֹ
"o" as in open	chataf-kamatz	חֲטַף-קָמָץ	◌ֳ
"eh" as in bed	segol	סֶגוֹל	◌ֶ
"eh" as in bed	chataf-segol	חֲטַף-סֶגוֹל	◌ֱ
"ei" as in eight (some people say "eh")	tzeirei	צֵירֵי	◌ֵ
"oo" as in moose	shuruk	שׁוּרֻק	וּ
"oo" as in moose	kubutz	קֻבּוּץ	◌ֻ

Notes